LIKE
LIVING STONES

LIKE
LIVING STONES

Reflections on some current ethical issues

by W. Pouwelse

PREMIER PUBLISHING
WINNIPEG

Pouwelse, W., 1928—
  Like living stones

  Bibliography: p.
  Includes index.
  ISBN 0-88756-030-X
  1. Christian ethics — Reformed authors.
2. Christian life — Reformed authors. I. Title.
BJ1251.P67 1985   241'.045732   C86-091005-9

First printing – 1985
Second printing – 1986
Third printing – 1989
Fourth printing – 1993

PREMIER PUBLISHING
ONE BEGHIN AVENUE, WINNIPEG, MANITOBA, CANADA R2J 3X5

PREFACE

In I Peter 2 the apostle admonishes his audience to live in such a way that the Name of God may be glorified. He calls Jesus Christ the cornerstone of the spiritual house, the ground and rock of our salvation. Thankful for this precious gift we have to offer our whole life as a spiritual sacrifice, acceptable to God through Jesus Christ.

Doing so, we will become like living stones in the spiritual house of which Jesus Christ is the cornerstone. In order to live in such a way, we have to face and to clear up many practical questions. Many issues in everyday life call for an answer. Ethical decisions have to be made. Not in every situation is it a clear cut matter which route we have to go. Many aspects have to be considered.

In this book I will try to help you come to grips with some current issues. On most of the topics I have published a series of articles in the Canadian Reformed Magazine, *CLARION.* As a result of the reactions received, I have decided to rework some of the material for publication in a book. The set-up of this book is such that it can be used either as reading material, or as an outline for discussion at the study societies. May it serve as a guideline for many discussions and give some food for thought in a turbulent world.

That we ourselves, LIKE LIVING STONES (cf. I Peter 2:5), may be built into a spiritual house, to be a holy priesthood, to offer spiritual sacrifices acceptable to God through Jesus Christ, is the sincere desire of

THE AUTHOR

Langley, BC   Fall 1985

CONTENTS

CHAPTER VII

The Borderline of Human Life

CHAPTER VIII

Test-tube Babies

CHAPTER IX

Organ Transplants

CHAPTER X

Child Abuse

CHAPTER XI

Capital Punishment

CHAPTER XII

Some Reflections on War and Disarmament

CHAPTER ONE

Marriage and Family Life

1. The basic stronghold

Family life is the cornerstone of our Christian society. It is in the family that children are confronted with authority for the first time. It is in the family that the groundwork is laid for their attitude and approach to life. The rule is that children follow the pattern of their parents' life and that they go one step further in the direction of their own preference. Exceptions exist and have always existed, but they only confirm the rule. Therefore we will focus first of all on the basic stronghold of society and the center of Christian education and training: the family.

In this first chapter we will pay special attention to the problems and questions of youngsters who are growing to maturity and who are preparing themselves for their future task and responsibility in family life. We will consider the position of the present generation of parents and their involvement in this process; we will have a look at the guidance and support they must give their teenagers and at the necessity of communication between the different generations.

We are living in a time in which customs and traditions are changing rapidly. We hear about a generation gap. It does not serve any purpose to deny the existence of such a gap. We had better try to analyze why some parents and children do not communicate. We all agree that it should not be that way. Therefore we will consider what can be done to cope with these problems. What can we do to prevent matters from getting worse, and how can we improve communication within the family?

Our young people are like a ship that has to go to sea. It must first go through the rough rolling waves near the coastline before it reaches calmer and deeper water. Sometimes a pilot is needed in order to leave the harbour safely. If the ship is wrecked on the rocks, it will never reach its destination, but if it passes the coastline, it comes into calmer water and can continue its trip without too much difficulty.

Parents have to be aware of the fact that their children need guidance, assistance, and advice — not to prevent them from becoming mature and independent, but to help them to pass the most turbulent part of their life.

In this chapter I will try to provide some help by discussing a number of problems and aspects of the process of coming to maturity.

Customs and traditions change, but the norm of the Word of God remains the same. Therefore we should try to make a distinction between changing customs and traditions, on the one hand, and the unchangeable and infallible Word of God and the norms set by Scripture, on the other hand.

Preparing for and growing to maturity often go together with preparing for marriage, via engagement. Therefore we will pay ample attention to this aspect.

The first question we have to consider is: Where do young people meet each other?

2. The first contacts

There are many ways to meet other young people and to make initial contacts. Sometimes we hear very nice, or rather unusual stories about how a husband and wife met each other for the first time.

In the past people did not have many opportunities to meet other people because they had to work all day long. They did not go to high school or have summer camps. Often the only place where they met others was at catechism class or young people's society, although even these were held in separate places most of the time. Regional meetings of the young people's societies were therefore an excellent opportunity for boys and girls to meet. Nowadays there are many occasions to make contacts. We should be thankful for many things which can be considered improvements. However, for getting a boyfriend or a girlfriend it is still very important where the young people meet each other.

Sometimes the question is asked: Are you supposed to tell your date right away, the first evening you go out, to which church you belong and to ask him or her about his or her faith? This is an important point and it brings us right to the centre of the issue at stake.

The answer should be: No, of course not. But don't get me wrong now. I do not suggest that this question is not important. On the contrary. You should know about those things before you go out or arrange a date.

Where do you meet other young people, and why do you go out together? Having a date is not just a matter of entertainment. It should at least be an attempt to see whether there is a basis for further contact. In trying to get better acquainted with someone, you have to find out the person's most important likes and dislikes. You talk about your work and about your hobbies and see how you can please one another. But one of the most important things should be what your attitude in life is: whether God is your Father and Jesus Christ your only Saviour. If you do not find out these things during the first encounter, what kind of things do you discuss then?

The question *where* you meet for the first time is important in this respect. If you meet each other at catechism classes or at young people's, you know about these things already.

Preparation for a marriage means to get used to each other, to see whether you can work and talk together and whether your characters really fit together. Most of these things you find out already while studying God's Word at young people's.

If you arrange a date with a boy or girl without knowing anything about the person's spiritual life, you must have met each other at a place and in circumstances where you had no opportunity to find out. Then there is even more reason to talk about these things as soon as possible.

It is quite well possible that you deem it inappropriate to discuss these matters, because the environment is not suitable, or because you are afraid that people will laugh at you. That should be a clear indication that you have chosen the wrong company.

Suppose you have a date, and you are ashamed to tell who your parents are, where they live, and what your father's job is. That would be embarrassing for your parents, wouldn't it? It would show that something is wrong in your relationship with your parents. When you start hiding or covering up the most important things in your life, you are starting off on the wrong foot. That will pose lots of problems later on.

It is important where you meet each other. This is true not only with respect to dating, it is a crucial point for making friends in general. That brings us to our next point.

3. Who are your friends?

We, as Christians, are not living on an island, far away from what is going on in the world. On the contrary. Too many of our young people get involved with alcohol and drugs. Especially in this respect we have to be careful that a generation gap does not prevent us from being on the alert.

In the past the pub was a place where Christians were not supposed to go and movies were a strictly forbidden area. Nowadays going to the pub or a restaurant seems to be very common and movies are brought into the house via T.V. That makes our young people vulnerable; they wonder what the difference is between watching T.V. and going to the movies. Excessive drinking is becoming a problem more and more, and young people wonder why they cannot go to the pub to have a drink there.

The use of so-called soft drugs is not something that remains unknown to them either. There is an increasing danger of having our young people involved in these things.

Therefore we have to consider the question: Where and how do you find your friends?

We are living in this world. We cannot go out of the world. We have to be a light on a candlestick and should give a clear testimony. In our daily job we have to work together with others, often unbelievers. We have to be prepared to defend our point of view and our faith. We have to resist all the attacks of the devil. We have to stand firm and to overcome all temptations. We are allowed to ask the Lord for His help and support when we have to fight against sin and temptation. However, in our recreation we should stay away from all these kinds of temptations.

Who are your friends? Where do you go when you want to relax? To relax means: to stop worrying and to be less active, not to be on the alert all the time. When you *go* to places where the service of the Lord is ignored — or even worse, where it is mocked — you cannot really relax.

There are only two options: either you have to fight all the time against the temptations of sin, and that will make your life unnecessarily difficult, or you will give in and lose your sense of the distinction between good and evil.

Let us not fool ourselves. Bad company, excessive drinking, and the use of drugs have led astray too many people. What we need is good communication between parents and children, open discussions to help each other and to assist each other. A communication defect makes things worse.

4. Communication defect

What do we mean by "communication," and what is a "communication defect?" The word *communication* means: to transfer information, feelings, opinions, and advice to one another.

Communication is a current topic. There are all kinds of specialists in communication techniques. Generally speaking, at least three conditions have to be met to achieve proper communication.

1. There has to be a transmitter, sending out information.
2. There must be a receiver, able to accept the information.
3. They have to be tuned-in to each other.

We can also put it this way, dealing with human beings: there has to be someone who speaks, someone who listens, and they have to understand each other's language. All three aspects are important, and if one of them is missing, there is no communication at all. Although this might seem to be obvious, it is often overlooked, and that has disastrous consequences.

Let us pay some attention to these three aspects.

There has to be someone who speaks. Do parents really speak with their children about their problems? We sometimes tend to blame the young people, stating that things are much worse now than they were in the past. But don't forget: today's youth is exactly the same as the youth of the past. They act and react in the way they have been brought up, and they try to go just one step further. Of course, that is the general rule. There are exceptions, but these exceptions existed in every generation. Also that is nothing new.

We can and should be very thankful for the many activities our young people have nowadays, but we must be careful not to treat all the young people the same. We should not blame the good guys for what the bad guys are doing, or blame the young people without asking what their parents are doing.

Do the parents really talk with their children? Do they try to understand their problems? Don't forget that our youngsters are growing up in a completely different society than most of the parents are familiar with.

Nowadays there is an increasing liberality in sexual relations. Do the parents speak with their children about these things, or do they leave it up to the schools to give education in this respect? Don't ignore the influence of what they hear from friends, colleagues, and the news media. In talking with young people about these things it becomes clear time and again how desperately they need the guidance and support of the parents. Sometimes the complaint is heard that they cannot talk at all with their parents about these things, because their parents consider them "dirty."

The first condition for communication is that there is someone who speaks. Of course, that counts for both sides. Not only are the parents supposed to speak; the children also have to come with their questions and speak about their problems. Communication is never a one way street.

That brings us to the second point, namely, that someone is listening. That seems to be even more difficult. Did you ever realize how hard it is to listen? It happens once in a while, on a homevisit by the elders, that someone very cautiously comes forward with a question or tries to bring a certain delicate point to the fore. The very eloquent visitor, having heard a few words, begins a long speech, without realizing what the real problem is. Now, the speech might be very interesting; everything the elder says may be true, but he misses the point. And the shy person shuts up and refrains from asking any further questions. There was no communication.

Many people are very quick in answering but very poor in listening. While a person is still speaking, they are already preparing their answer, and therefore they do not hear the rest of what the speaker says, thus missing the crux of the matter. The result is that, at best, two persons are speaking, one at a time — or even worse — both at the same time, while no one is listening.

There are interesting books available on the subject of active listening, but reading a book does not help as long as we do not practise what we have read. For real communication it is necessary that we listen to each other with the intention of understanding what the other has in mind. Only after we have understood the meaning and intention of the speaker, can we give an answer that is to the point and makes sense.

The third condition, mentioned above, is that the transmitter and the receiver are tuned-in to each other, or, in other words, that they use the same language, that they understand each other. Especially in our society young people often have the idea that they are not being understood. The expression, "Forget about it!" is often a sign of frustration. The person has the feeling that the other didn't get the point. He gives up. That causes a communication defect. That a young person says: "My parents do not understand my problem. I can't talk with them about it. They are living in such a completely different world and their ideas are so completely different. I can't explain to them how I feel" — is a serious thing.

We can and should not defend everything that happens nowadays among the young people. Far from it. But parents should at least try to understand what the problems are and how their children feel. Ignoring reality only makes things worse.

5. Mixed couples

A point of special attention is what is often referred to as "mixed couples": a date, an engagement, or a marriage in which one of the two is a believer and the other is not.

A question often asked is: What is wrong with being engaged to someone who is not a member of the church? We do not have very much choice. Especially in small congregations young people can have difficulty finding a friend. Sometimes they even consider it a matter of evangelism to have a friend from outside the church. You never know whether you can bring someone to Christ. Does not the apostle Paul himself say in I Corinthians 7:12-16: ". . . if any brother has a wife who is an unbeliever, and she consents to live with him, he should not divorce her. If any woman has a husband who is an unbeliever, and he consents to live with her, she should not divorce him. For the unbelieving husband is consecrated through his wife, and the unbelieving wife is consecrated through her husband. Otherwise your children would be unclean, but as it is they are holy."

That seems to make sense. If you leave each other free, if the other consents to living together without hindering the partner in serving the Lord, what is wrong with that? The unbelieving husband is consecrated through his wife and the unbelieving wife is consecrated through her husband. And the children are holy. That is the reasoning we often hear.

If we reason along this line, it even appears preferable to seek a date, a boyfriend or a girlfriend, outside the church. That is evangelism; that is the way you can bring others to Christ.

Such reasoning is wrong. Evangelism is an important thing and we should try to bring others to Christ, wherever we can. All kinds of methods can be used. But we should not use marriages or engagements as tools of evangelism.

It is an incorrect use of the Bible to quote the above-mentioned text to defend such a case. The apostle does not speak about dating, engagement, or a preparation for a marriage. What he refers to is a couple who married while they were both unbelievers. Later one of them became a Christian. What were they supposed to do now? Break up the marriage, because the partner was not (or not yet) a believer? No, the apostle says. If the one becomes a Christian, the other should be given time to think it over, to make up his mind. Don't rush and don't push too hard. Don't separate from each other all of a sudden. If the other agrees to stay together and in the meantime leaves you free to serve the Lord, you should stay together as long as possible. You never know; perhaps God will bring the other to Christ as well. It took you a while to accept the gospel; therefore bear patiently with your partner. If the other becomes a hindrance to your serving the Lord, if he no longer accepts your serving the Lord, if he becomes hostile, you may be forced to separate, for Christ's sake. But don't do it too hastily.

This has nothing to do with getting engaged to someone who is not a believer. For that situation the apostle has another message. To those who are believers and who are about to make an arrangement or a choice to get married, the apostle writes in II Corinthians 6:14-18: "Do not be mismated with unbelievers. For what partnership have righteousness and iniquity? Or what fellowship has light with darkness? What accord has Christ with Belial? Or what has a believer in common with an unbeliever? What agreement has the temple of God with idols? For we are the temple of the living God; as God said, 'I will live in them and move among them, and I will be their God, and they shall be My people. Therefore come out from them, and be separate from them, says the LORD, and touch nothing unclean; then I will welcome you, and you shall be My sons and daughters, says the LORD Almighty.' "

That should be our attitude. "Do not be mismated with unbelievers."

I'm not saying that all forms of cooperation with unbelievers are impossible per se. If that were the case we would have to go out of this world. In our daily work we have to work together. That can create problems. We must defend our point of view and our faith wherever necessary. Sometimes we must fight. In other instances we will have to withdraw, because it is impossible for us to comply with certain rules or regulations. A job can have requirements which we, as Christians, cannot meet. But still we have our task and mandate in this world.

However, in the married state husband and wife have to be one in faith; they have to support each other in every respect. They have to live together in holiness, according to the Word of God. In I Corinthians 6:19 the apostle Paul says: "Do you not know that your body is a temple of the Holy Spirit within you, which you have from God? You are not your own; you were bought with a price. So glorify God in your body."

A temple of the Holy Spirit is what we are supposed to be. It is clear that you cannot begin a relationship when you are not one in Christ.

In the previous section we dealt with the necessity of communication. That is extremely important. These matters have to be discussed right from the beginning. When young people go steady for a long time, it can be very difficult to keep the relationship pure and holy according to the Word of God. Decisions have to be made; temptations have to be overcome and resisted. It is very important to be one in faith and to know and agree about what the Lord asks from you. Therefore a couple should discuss these matters right from the beginning, or, rather, you should know about a person's relation with the Lord before you establish a relationship with him or her.

Too often these matters are postponed. "We will talk about it later. It's not necessary just yet. Don't worry; we will solve this problem. Because we really love each other, we will be able to straighten it out when the time comes."

But don't forget: faith is not something you can give to someone else or something you can agree on of your own accord. As a relationship develops, you grow closer, and it will be more difficult to break it up later, if it becomes clear that the other does not become a believer.

We have to be aware of a danger in two directions. It is possible that someone, to avoid problems with relatives, agrees to join the church,

17

without being convinced. That is not right, and it is not honest and fair either. No one should become a member of the church to satisfy others. To join the church should always be a matter of personal faith and conviction. It is also possible that the believing partner gives in and leaves the church. If you are not able to wait with building a relationship until you are sure about someone's relation to the Lord, it will appear to be impossible to break up the relationship later when you do not agree about joining the church.

Too often it happens that these matters are dealt with in a rush, without really straightening them out. The consequences become manifest later.

Of course, there are also cases where someone joins the church and becomes a faithful member, even an example for others. Such people may see the hand of the Lord in their life. When people, from whatever origin they may be, join the church because they believe in Jesus Christ, they are full-fledged members of the church. Sometimes they are even better members than those who have never thought about their membership. We have to be humble and we have to acknowledge that some are members simply because they are too lazy and too indifferent to do something else; they take it for granted and they don't like any trouble, but they are not interested or involved in church life at all. We are not talking about numbers; it does not matter how many or how few cases like this there are. They exist! Let us therefore not look down on members who joined the church just a couple of years before they got married.

There is one thing we should keep in mind, and that is that membership of the church has to be a matter of priority. I am convinced that those who joined the church before they got married and who became faithful members of the church are the ones who discussed these things right from the beginning and often agreed beforehand that they could marry only if the one voluntarily and with conviction would join the church so that they would become one in faith.

6. Prayer

The time of engagement is a time of preparation for marriage. The two people try to become better acquainted with each other. They have to learn how to get along — not only at a party or during a nice evening of entertainment, but also when they have to face problems and when they disagree. They have to fight together against the temptations of sin. They have to accept each other's weak points, shortcomings, and bad habits. They have to learn how to share joy and sorrow.

Nowadays when young people are together, they feel freer than in the past. They are no longer so shy, especially not in conversation. In the "world" we see another extreme. There seem to be no secrets at all. The slogan is: Do just what you like. As long as you don't hurt someone else, either physically or spiritually, it is alright. Therefore it is very important that young people develop a sound relationship in another direction. They really need the strength and guidance of the Holy Spirit to be able to stand firm in all kinds of temptations.

When young people are together, discussing their plans for the future, preparing for the married state, getting acquainted with each other, they should also make it a custom to pray together. Some consider that to be strange. Imagine, a young couple, not yet married, praying together? But don't forget that the time of engagement is a preparation for the married state. After the wedding you have to do everything together. Bringing before the throne of God everything in your life can be a great help in living in holiness before the Lord and in overcoming temptations during your engagement. To pray together brings you closer together in your love for one another and makes you one in the Lord. It will give you strength to stand firm and to keep your bodies holy temples of the Lord.

Isn't it strange that so many people anticipate their married state in the way they live together during their engagement and are scared or too shy to pray together? It should be just the other way around. Praying together belongs to the necessary spiritual preparations for marriage.

7. The wedding ceremony

The married state is an institution of the LORD. He has said from the beginning: It is not good that man should be alone; I will make him a helper fit for him (Genesis 2:18). The Form for the Solemnization of Marriage puts it this way: "Since the Lord forbids immorality, each man should have his own wife and each woman should have her own husband, so that our bodies may be preserved as temples of the Holy Spirit and we may glorify God in our body." Therefore shall a man leave his father and his mother and he shall cleave to his wife, and they shall become one flesh (Genesis 2:24 and Ephesians 5:32).

The married state is an institution of the LORD. Marriage is basically an agreement between two persons to live together as husband and wife, according to the ordinance of the LORD. It is in the first place something in which the parents have to be involved. The young people will leave their respective parents to become one flesh and to have their own family. That has to be done with the consent of their parents. A marriage is not a decision of the church, nor a pronouncement of the civil government. It is, in the first place, a family matter. However, the church and the civil government each do have their own responsibility in this respect.

When a child is born, it has to be registered in the files of the civil government and in the administrative records of the church. A child does not exist because it is legally registered; it has to be registered because it exists. The same thing applies to marriage. A marriage has to be registered. In some countries that can take place only at City Hall. In Canada a marriage can be legally registered by a church minister who is registered by the provincial government for that purpose.

The minister does not "marry" the couple. No, the couple, in the presence and with the consent of the parents, marry each other; the minister fulfils the legally necessary steps to register this marriage. He pronounces them husband and wife because they are husband and wife.

The couple has to declare publicly that they have accepted and do accept each other as husband and wife. They have to give their vows publicly, because their married state has consequences also for their position in public life.

During the wedding ceremony they have to promise that they will live according to the commandments of the LORD. In the Form for the Solemnization of Marriage it says: Do you promise . . . to live with him/her in holiness, according to the holy gospel?

According to the laws of the country, a marriage can easily be dissolved by a divorce, but, according to the Word of God, husband and wife have to stay together. They promise never to forsake one another. They have to live together "until death will part them" (as the Form puts it).

The wedding ceremony in the church is not a sacrament. It is a private meeting of the family, with a minister conducting the ceremony. In this respect the question can be asked whether a marriage can be solemnized when one of the parties is not a member of the church.

In the Form for the Solemnization of Marriage one of the questions that has to be asked of the couple is: Do you promise to live with him/her according to the holy gospel? Before this question can be asked and answered honestly and in all fairness, it has to be clear that bride and groom understand what that means. They promise that they not only are willing to live according to the gospel, but that they also will guide and assist one another and help each other to live in that manner. That is a commitment and a responsibility, even more comprehensive than the promise given upon confession of faith.

It is impossible and not fair and honest to ask this question, to expect an answer, or to answer it, if the persons involved do not really know what it means. Therefore someone who is not able or willing to commit himself to serve the Lord and to join the church as a communicant member, cannot answer this question. We can also put it the other way: someone who is able to answer this question honestly and in all fairness should be able to join the church as a communicant member and should act accordingly.

Therefore the question is not, in the first place, whether the marriage of a member of the church and an unbeliever can be solemnized in the church, but whether the persons involved are able to answer the questions.

This brings us to another point, and that is what to do when one of the two is a noncommunicant member.

8. A wedding of noncommunicant members

The main point of what has been said in the previous section about marriage to someone who is an unbeliever also applies, to a certain extent, to noncommunicant members. The real question is not whether a marriage can be solemnized in the church, but whether the bride and the groom are able to answer the questions. Are they prepared to make such a pledge and commitment? They have to promise to live according to the commandments of the LORD. They have to take care of each other and help each other to live according to the holy gospel.

There are only two options, as far as I can see. Either a person is ready to answer the questions and to accept the full responsibility — but then he should also be able to make public profession of faith — or he is not ready, not mature enough, to make profession of faith; he needs further instruction to understand what the Word of God means and he is not yet ready to commit his whole life to the service of the Lord — but then he must also be considered unable to answer the questions in the Form for the Solemnization of Marriage.

I cannot see how someone can make the commitment asked in the Form for Marriage, while he/she cannot make public profession of faith. We have to be careful that someone does not make such a pledge simply for the sake of the nice, impressive marriage ceremony, without understanding the real meaning and impact of such a commitment. That would not be honest and fair.

We have to put the matters in the proper perspective, and we have to set the right priorities. A full commitment to the service of the Lord has to come first. A person cannot and should not take the responsibility for a family and, consequently, for the raising of children, as long as he/she is not mature enough to become a full-fledged member of the church.

Of course, there can be the situation where someone is ready to make public profession of faith, but where the date of this public profession is still a couple of months away because of the program set for the preconfession class. It would be better in such a case to postpone the wedding until the profession of faith has taken place, than to make an exception to the rule that profession of faith must be made first. If there are insurmountable objections to postponing the wedding, it would be preferable to ask for an earlier date for that particular person's public profession of faith, than to have the wedding first. However, what are "insurmountable objections"? Probably a forced marriage? That is the next point I should like to discuss.

9. Forced marriages

It happens from time to time that two young people live together during their engagement in such a way that they become expectant parents even before they are married. That is a sad and deplorable situation. It is clear to everyone that they have transgressed the commandments of the LORD. It is often considered a shame and a disgrace for the family, especially for the parents. It creates a lot of gossip within the congregation and outside of it.

Still, we have to say more about it than just that. The Bible teaches us clearly that sexual intercourse is inseparably connected with the married state. Every form of promiscuity or premarital relations stands in violation of the commandments of the LORD.

When a boy and a girl are engaged for a long time before they get married, it can become difficult for them to fight against the temptation to anticipate their marriage. Sometimes through weakness they fall into sin. We should not defend this and we have to call sin *sin*.

Lots of people deny or ignore these rules. It is becoming more and more common that young people live together as husband and wife. Sex is considered a form of entertainment. Everyone is free to do just what he likes. If two people agree to be together, it is no one else's business.

Let us not close our eyes to the reality of this. Our young people are growing up in a world in which the norms of God's Word are ignored. The norm for human life is what pleases man. As long as you do not hurt or harm anybody else, you are right. What makes people happy is what is good. That is the humanistic attitude of today. And it does not leave our young people untouched. Parents should discuss these matters with their children. It has to be understood that a so-called "free" relationship is a matter of sin.

It seems to be a different case when people are engaged and have made a firm commitment to stay together. Sometimes the question is asked: When we have made a solemn promise to live together for our whole life, why shouldn't we have sexual intercourse? Doesn't that belong to the preparation for the married state? We have to know each other in every respect. And, moreover, although we are not officially married, before the Lord we are married, and we have made a pledge never to forsake one another.

This question is sometimes asked in all seriousness and the persons concerned really believe they are right. Still we must answer these questions with a definite "no." The Bible calls the married state "to become one flesh," and God's Word teaches us clearly that sexual relations cannot and may not be separated from the married state.

There is, however, one aspect we should keep in mind when we talk about forced marriages, and that is what the Word of God says about this matter. When we speak about a forced marriage we are referring to a situation in which a baby is expected before the couple is married. The Bible speaks in a different way. The question whether a man has to marry a girl, whether he should be "forced" to marry her, does not depend on whether she becomes pregnant. The Bible teaches us that the simple fact that a couple has a sexual relationship obligates them to marry. We read about it in Exodus 22:16: "If a man seduces a virgin who is not betrothed, and lies with her, he shall give the marriage present for her and make her his wife." In Deuteronomy 22:28 we read: "If a man meets a virgin who is not betrothed, and seizes her and lies with her, and they are found, then the man who lay with her shall give to the father of the young woman fifty shekels of silver, and she shall be his wife, because he has violated her; he may not put her away all his days."

This shows us clearly that we can speak of a forced marriage, whether the girl becomes pregnant or not. By virtue of the fact that they have had a sexual relationship, they are obligated to be publicly united in the married state.

This is one Biblical aspect we have to keep in mind. Another point is this: in the Old Testament severe punishments were sometimes executed. In some cases of fornication and adultery, capital punishment was used. It is therefore remarkable that in a situation involving premarital relations the Bible (only?) says: they have to be united in the married state; they are not allowed to forsake each other.

That must have consequences in two directions. Sometimes a "forced marriage" is considered to be the worst thing that can happen in a family. However, it may have been a matter of falling into sin in a moment of weakness during a continuous fight against sin. We do not condone such a sin. Not at all. But it is sad that these young people sometimes get to hear from other young members of the congregation, "You should have been more careful. You could have prevented this by using the pill or some other contraceptive means. It will never happen with us!" That hurts them the most.

When young people use the pill or other methods of birth control — or rather, birth prevention — it is not a matter of "falling into sin" in a moment of weakness, but deliberately living in sin. Let us not fool ourselves, thinking that such things do not happen among Christians. An open discussion with our young people will reveal a different reality. Fortunately, many are fighting this decay in morality, this transgression of God's commandments. It is these young people who are upset about what is going on and who once in a while open up to express their frustrations.

A so-called forced marriage is a sad matter. It has to be confessed before the countenance of the Lord as sin. But, as we have learned from the Word of God (in Exodus 22 and Deuteronomy 22), the Bible speaks about a forced marriage in all instances where there has been intercourse, whether it has caused pregnancy or not. I am afraid that we would have many more "forced marriages" if we applied these Biblical norms. Let us not forget that those who break up a relationship after they have had sexual intercourse are more guilty. They are committing a sin which, in the Old Testament, was punished with death.

We should not treat all people alike. We are very glad that many of our young people are fighting the good fight to keep their bodies as holy temples of the Lord. We should encourage them in their struggle in the midst of a world laughing at such an attitude. We should not blame them for what others are doing. But to prevent things from getting worse, we should at the same time have an open eye for what is going on. We have to be aware of the danger which is threatening our young people. Many have fallen victim to a worldly attitude, and only an open discussion between parents and children can help in this respect.

10. Unwed mothers

In the previous section we considered what the Bible says about "forced marriage." It means: the man has to marry the woman. The boy is not allowed to leave the girl.

There is, however, one exception we have not discussed yet. We have already quoted Exodus 22:16, but now we should also read what it says in the next verse. In Exodus 22:17 we read: "If her father utterly refuses to give her to him, he shall pay money equivalent to the marriage present for virgins." In other words: the girl's father has the right to refuse the boy's request to marry his daughter. That does not take away the obligation of the man who had a relationship with her. He has to live up to the financial consequences in paying a dowry. But he cannot have her as his wife. They will not be married.

In our present situation it means that through a sinful life, through a very short relationship with a certain boy, it can happen that a girl becomes pregnant, but that there still is good reason not to get married to him.

An engagement is a relationship which serves as a preparation for the married state. Such a commitment should not be broken lightly. In the married state husband and wife have to live together, also when there are problems, when they sometimes even disagree on certain points or when they have a little fight together. During their engagement, the young people must try to understand and to accept each other, also in their weaknessess and shortcomings. But an engagement is not a marriage. Even when they have anticipated their marriage in having sexual relations, they still are not married. Especially when they find out that they do not fit together spiritually, that they are not and cannot become one in Christ, they should break up their relationship rather than begin a marriage in which they cannot really be one in the Lord.

The same counts when a girl expects a baby. The rule is that they get married as soon as possible. They have lived together as a married couple and they should ask for the official registration of this relationship. But the Bible mentions one exception in Exodus 22, as we saw. The girl's father can refuse a man's request to get married to his daughter. That means that, if the man who has procreated the baby is an unbeliever or a person who makes a marriage in the Lord impossible, the girl had better accept becoming an unwed mother, rather than to be married to a man with whom she cannot be one in Christ.

It is a sad consequence, and we should not think too lightly about it. A sin sometimes has consequences which cannot be undone. Although the relationship was an anticipation of the married state, they were not married yet. Also in this case the instruction of II Corinthians 6:14 is valid: "Do not mismate with an unbeliever."

One sin can never be an excuse for another. It is better for a girl to live in a close relationship to the Lord as an unwed mother, than to join in the married state with a man with whom she cannot be one in Christ and who will be a hindrance in her relationship with the Lord and in the raising of her child in the fear of His Name.

Confessed sins are forgiven sins, although the consequences may be felt for the rest of one's life. We know that in obedience to the Lord we can count on His help and guidance, also in a difficult situation. He never forsakes those who come to Him in true faith and repentance.

And we, as Christians, should support such people, remembering what the apostle says in Galatians 6:1: "If a man [or a woman] is overtaken in any trespass, you who are spiritual should restore him [or her] in a spirit of gentleness. Look to yourself, lest you too be tempted. Bear one another's burdens, and so fulfil the law of Christ."

CHAPTER TWO

Marriage and Divorce

1. An old phenomenon

In the previous chapter we considered various aspects of coming together and getting married. However, not every couple that gets married lives "happily ever after," even if they are both communicant members of the church and enter holy wedlock with good intentions and proper preparations. Unfortunately, also among Christians marriage problems occur, and even separation and divorce are not unheard of.

What should our attitude be towards this? What stand must the office-bearers take? Are disciplinary measures required, and, if so, which ones and for what period of time? Can someone who has been divorced remarry, or is reconciliation the only option? Does someone who has been divorced have to remain single for the rest of his/her life, even if he/she is not to blame for the failure of the marriage?

No one should be surprised that separation and divorce are current issues also among Christians. We are not immune to what is going on in the world. Denying this reality is burying one's head in the sand. According to statistics, one out of every three or four marriages ends in separation or divorce within five years. That is the average in the world, and in some areas it is even worse. Let us not fool ourselves, thinking that this development will leave the Christian community untouched.

Moreover, marriage breakup, marriage failure, separation, and divorce are not brand-new issues. They have existed throughout the ages. Already in the Old Testament we can read about it. In Deuteronomy 24 we find regulations for the people of Israel. Jesus Himself says in Matthew 19 that "for your hardness of heart Moses allowed you to divorce your wives, but from the beginning it was not so." A man should not put away his wife; there should be no divorce or separation. But still it exists. We, as Christians, should not ignore or deny the reality of this. We should face it and try to find the proper way to deal with it.

We should not approve or play down sin, but we should not close our eyes to its consequence either. Although a girl should not become pregnant before she is married, there are "forced marriages" and there are "unwed mothers." We have to deal with them in a Christian manner and according to Galatians 6:1: "If a man [or a woman] is overtaken in any trespass, you who are spiritual should restore him [or her] in a spirit of gentleness. Look to yourself, lest you too be tempted."

It is the same with separation and divorce. It is against the will of God. What God has joined together, let not man put asunder. But as long as we are living in a sinful world, waiting for the renewal of all things when our Lord Jesus Christ comes back upon the clouds of heaven, we have to face the consequences of a broken human society, even a broken Christian society. The destructive power of sin is evident and we have to contend with it.

In this chapter we will consider our attitude in this respect. We first must search the Scriptures to see and hear what the Bible says about it. Then we have to face the reality of everyday life and apply the norm of the Word of God to our way of life and our approach to this kind of problem. Christian ethics means to apply the revelation of God's Word to everyday life in all its changing circumstances. Changing circumstances may ask for different measures, but the norm, the standard, the Law of the LORD our God, remains unchanged and unchangeable. In Deuteronomy 24 we read about "hardness of hearts." Moses had to deal with it. Our Lord Jesus Christ spoke about it in Matthew 19, and we have to deal with it as well.

2. Some definitions

Dealing with an issue like this, we should try as much as possible to avoid confusion by using expressions which are not clearly defined. Different people can use the same words but still be talking about completely different things. That causes misunderstanding, confusion, and sometimes conflicts. Therefore it might be worthwhile to make some introductory remarks about certain expressions which I am going to use quite frequently.

When I use the word *separation,* I am referring to a situation in which a husband and wife, although legally married, do not actually live together as husband and wife.

We can distinguish three different "types" of separation, depending on the reason why people do not live together.

First, there is the situation where both parties agree to stay away from each other. Such a separation can be a temporary measure to prevent things from getting worse and to work towards restoration of peace and unity in the family.

In the second place, separation can be the result of the fact that one party has left the other. That can be with bad intentions, or it can result when the other party creates an unbearable situation, or any of a number of other reasons.

In the third place, a separation can be the result of a judicial verdict. A judge can grant the request of one of the parties and deny the other the right to enter the home where they used to live together.

Divorce refers to a legal and judicial verdict by which a marriage has been definitively dissolved. It may be necessary in certain situations to make a distinction between a *legal* divorce and the still-existing *Biblical* obligation to stay together and to reconcile or to remain single without the possibility of a remarriage. A judicial statement of a worldly judge does not automatically dissolve a marriage before the Lord. The civil law cannot change the Biblical rule. What the Lord has joined together man should not put asunder. We have to obey the civil government as the authority given by the Lord, but at the same time we have to be obedient to God rather than to men. Moreover, the government allows people to dissolve their marriage by a divorce, but the government does not force us to use this option. In other words: the government can relieve us of the obligations and duties of marriage according to the civil law, but the government can never relieve us of the obligations we have according to the law of the Lord.

The terms *adultery* and *fornication* also need some special attention. In the seventh commandment we read, according to the RSV translation of the Bible: "You shall not commit adultery." It is clear that this commandment forbids all impure sexual relations, not just the breakup of a marriage. Therefore it might be worthwhile to note that this translation does not use the word *fornication* but the word *adultery*.

The word *fornication* comes from a word that originally referred to the underground vaults and arches in the old city of Rome, in which perverse actions took place (fornix means: vault or arch). In contemporary English, fornication means a sexual act between two persons not married to each other, as when both of them are unmarried. It is clear that such an act is forbidden by the seventh commandment. However, our Bible translation does not use the word *fornication* but *adultery*.

With the word *adultery* we have to distinguish between the original meaning, its contemporary English meaning, and its Biblical or confessional meaning.

The original meaning of the word *adulterate* is to mix together or, more specifically, to debase or currupt by adding foreign or baser material. In contemporary English we still use the word *adulterate* in this sense; e.g. when a farmer adds water to milk we say that the milk has been adulterated with water. In the same way, wine can be adulterated with some other inferior additions. However, the word *adultery* is used in contemporary English almost exclusively for sexual relations between a married person and someone who is not his or her spouse. Therefore in our everyday language the difference between *fornication* and *adultery* is that with the former the parties are unmarried and with the latter at least one of them is married.

The Biblical or confessional meaning of the word *adultery* is much broader and more comprehensive. The seventh commandment is certainly not given for married couples only. It has a meaning for each and everyone. It refers back to the original meaning of the word *adulterate*. We should not mix the pure and beautiful relationship, instituted by the LORD and inherent to the married state, with any impure, foreign, or base relation. We should not debase or corrupt the wonderful gift of the LORD in the sexual relation between husband and wife with a strange or impure element.

28

This Biblical meaning is clearly explained in Lord's Day 41 of the Heidelberg Catechism, where we read: "What does the seventh commandment teach us? That all unchastity is accursed of God; and that we must, therefore, detest it from the heart, and live a chaste and continent life both within and outside the holy wedlock." We read further: "Does God in this commandment forbid nothing more than adultery and similar shameful sins?" and the answer is: "Since we, body and soul, are temples of the Holy Spirit, it is God's will that we keep ourselves pure and holy. Therefore He forbids all unchaste acts, gestures, words, thoughts, desires, and whatever may entice us to unchastity."

It is perfectly clear that the seventh commandment is not given for married people only but that it applies to each and everyone and has an impact on our whole life. Jesus Christ put it this way in Matthew 5:28: "But I say to you that everyone who looks at a woman lustfully has already committed adultery with her in his heart."

After this excursion about linguistic implications, we first turn our attention to what the Bible teaches about divorce.

3. Biblical starting-point

When we discuss our attitude and our response to separation and divorce, we take our starting point in what we read in Matthew 19:3-9. "And the Pharisees came up to Him and tested Him by asking, 'Is it lawful to divorce one's wife for any cause?' He answered, 'Have you not read that He who made them from the beginning made them male and female,' and said, 'For this reason a man shall leave his father and mother and be joined to his wife, and the two shall become one flesh?' So they are no longer two but one flesh. What therefore God has joined together, let not man put asunder.' They said to Him, 'Why then did Moses command one to give a certificate of divorce, and to put her away?' He said to them, 'For the hardness of heart Moses allowed you to divorce your wives, but from the beginning it was not so. And I say to you: Whoever divorces his wife, except for unchastity, and marries another, commits adultery.' "

The most striking part in this Scripture passage is Jesus' assurance that it is God who has joined together husband and wife in the holy married state. According to the ordinance of God they are no longer two but one flesh, and therefore man should not put asunder what God has joined together.

There should be no such thing as separation or divorce. That is our starting-point. It should not happen. It is sin. From the beginning it was not so. Only after we have stated and accepted the right norm and standard, can we talk about these matters in the proper way. We also learn from these words of our supreme Master and teacher that sin exists and that we have to deal with it. We are confronted every day with the "hardness of heart" of sinful man and its consequences.

In Matthew 19 reference is made to Deuteronomy 24. There Moses gave regulations for divorce and separation. We read in Deuteronomy

24:1-5: "When a man takes a wife and marries her, if then she finds no favour in his eyes because he has found some indecency in her, and he writes her a bill of divorce and puts it in her hand and sends her out of his house, and she departs out of his house, and if she goes and becomes another man's wife, and the latter husband dislikes her and writes her a bill of divorce and puts it in her hand and sends her out of his house, or if the latter husband dies, who took her to be his wife, then her former husband, who sent her away, may not take her again as his wife, after she has been defiled; for that is an abomination to the LORD, and you shall not bring guilt upon the land which the LORD your God gives you for an inheritance" (RSV translation).

We find a remarkable difference between the RSV and the KJV. The KJV has: "When a man hath taken a wife, and married her, and it comes to pass that she find no favour in his eyes, because he hath found some uncleanness in her: then let him write her a bill of divorcement, and give it in her hand, and send her out of his house. And when she is departed out of his house, she may go and be another man's wife. And if the latter husband hate her, and write her a bill of divorcement, and giveth it in her hand, and sendeth her out of his house; or if the latter husband die, which took her to be his wife; her former husband, which sent her away, may not take her again to be his wife, after that she is defiled; for that is an abomination before the LORD: and thou shalt not cause the land to sin, which the LORD thy God giveth thee for an inheritance."

It is important to notice the difference, because the explanation of this Scripture portion depends on the translation. According to the KJV Moses says: "When a man hath . . . found some uncleanness in her: let him write a bill of divorcement . . . and send her out of his house." In the RSV we do not find a period at the end of verse one, but a comma. This seemingly minor thing is very important for the meaning of the text. We have to make a few linguistic remarks to get to the point. In the RSV verse one is a so-called "if clause" (or a subordinate adverbial clause). The main clause of verses 1-4 is "When a man takes a wife and marries her, if . . . (verses 1,2,3) then the former husband . . . may not take her as his wife."

What is the practical consequence of these rather technical linguistic remarks? According to the KJV, verse one gives a rule for a man to send away his wife with a certificate of divorce. According to the RSV, Moses says only that, if a man has sent away his wife, he cannot take her again as his wife after she has been married to another man.

I consider (as many theologians do) the RSV translation better here. In Deuteronomy 24:1-4 Moses does not "give permission" to write a certificate of divorce. He only puts restriction on an existing practice. He does not say: "Let a man send away his wife," but rather: "If a man has sent away his wife, he cannot take her back again when it pleases him."

We should also take careful note of what Jesus says in Matthew 19:8. The Pharisees asked Him: "Why then did Moses command one to give a certificate of divorce, and put her away?" Jesus did not take over the suggestion of a commandment to send away, but he answered: "For the

30

hardness of heart Moses allowed you to divorce your wives . . . . " It makes quite a difference whether Moses *allowed* the people to do something or *commanded* them to do so.

Apparently Moses was speaking about the existing situation and custom in Israel and the surrounding nations to give a certificate of divorce. Moses did not abruptly put an end to this custom, in the same way as the custom of having more than one wife could continue. But restrictions were made to avoid futher abuse of this custom and to put certain limitations on it.

4. More about Deuteronomy 24

We have to say more about Deuteronomy 24. Verse one speaks about "some indecency" (RSV) or "some uncleanness" (KJV). Other translations say: "If he finds something he does not like with her." What is meant by that? It certainly does not refer to adultery! In Leviticus 20:10 and in Deuteronomy 22:22-27 we read that in the event of adultery both the man and the woman had to be put to death. Therefore, if a man found out that his wife had committed adultery, he would never send her away with a certificate of divorce. She had to be put to death — she as well as the man with whom she had committed adultery. Apparently Deuteronomy 24 refers to something else. Most likely the original meaning was a physical defect or infirmity of hers which he did not know about before the wedding. Later this ground for divorce received a much broader application; it was sometimes abused in terrible ways. According to some rabbis it was even possible for a man to send his wife away if he did not like her cooking or the way she was dressed. It is against the background of this abuse of Deuteronomy 24 that Jesus said in Matthew 19: " . . . from the beginning it was not so. And I say to you: whoever divorces his wife, except for unchastity, and marries another, commits adultery."

There are two more restrictions mentioned in Deuteronomy 22 with respect to writing a certificate of divorce and sending away a wife, and both show us that Deuteronomy 24 does not "open" a door for divorce but rather puts a restriction on an existing custom.

In Deuteronomy 22:19 we read about a man who falsely has accused his wife of having had sexual relations with someone else before the day of her wedding. If his accusation is proven to be false, then the man has to pay a fine to his father-in-law as a rehabilitation of the name and honour of his wife, and he is not allowed to send her away all his days.

In Deuteronomy 22:29 we read about a man who has had a sexual relation with a girl while they both were unmarried. In such a case the man has to marry the girl. It is what we would call a "forced marriage." Regardless of whether the girl becomes pregnant or not, he has to marry her and he is not allowed to send her away all his days.

In both cases a restriction is made to the apparently well-known custom of sending away a wife with a certificate of divorce. In both cases "he is not allowed to send her away all his days." He can never use the "opening" of Deuteronomy 24 to get rid of her. The Old Testament does not encourage the use of divorce but rather puts restraints on an existing custom.

Now that we have seen how the Old Testament speaks about divorce and what our Lord Jesus Christ says about it in Matthew 19, let us pay attention to what the attitude of the church was during the time of the New Testament.

5. Historical developments

The early Christian Church has always been very critical of divorce. A divorce was generally accepted only if adultery was committed by one of the partners. However, a remarriage of either of the two persons was mostly considered unacceptable. After a separation or a divorce parties either had to reconcile or stay unmarried. This point of view was closely related with the overestimation of the unmarried state, "celibacy" in the Roman Catholic Church. According to Roman Catholic doctrine, divorce is still not permitted, even after sexual unfaithfulness of one of the parties, unless the pope himself annuls the marriage.

After the Reformation it became commonly accepted that at least two legitimate reasons could be brought forward for divorce, namely, the sexual unfaithfulness of one of the partners and the reason mentioned in I Corinthians 7:15. The Westminster Confession goes even farther. We read in Chapter 24, Article 5: "In the case of adultery after marriage, it is lawful for the innocent party to sue for divorce: and, after the divorce, to marry another, as if the offending party were dead." Article 6 of the same chapter adds: "Nothing but adultery, or such wilful desertion as can in no way be remedied by the church or civil magistrate, is cause sufficient of dissolving the bond of marriage."

Apparently the Westminster Confession recognizes not only adultery and the reason mentioned in I Corinthians 7:15 as legitimate reasons for divorce, but also "such wilful desertion as can in no way be remedied by the church or civil magistrate."

About this last point there has been, and still is, a difference of opinion among believing Christians. The well-known Prof. G. Voetius considered wilful desertion a legitimate reason for divorce. The Reformed Churches, as far as I know, have never made a clear statement about this matter. The General Synods of Utrecht 1923 and Middelburg 1933 refused to make a statement, because — they said — "Scripture does not absolutely unequivocally speak" in this matter.

In Reformed circles separation is often accepted in cases of wilful desertion and other cases which "can in no way be remedied by the church or civil magistrate." It is accepted as an outlet for unbearable tensions. However, about a complete divorce and the possibility of remarriage unanimity does not exist.

6. A covenant relationship

When we consider the value of a Christian marriage and the question of divorce, we must keep in mind in the first place that marriage is a covenant relationship. The world treats marriage as a voluntary social contract which gives legal status to the relationship and more protection to the children, but which can be dissolved at any time if both partners agree. We as believers recognize that marriage is much more than that.

A marriage should always be a marriage "in the LORD." It has everything to do with the service of the LORD and with His covenant. In Malachi 2:10,11, we read how the LORD admonishes His people. "Have we not all one Father? Has not one God created us? Why then are we faithless to one another, profaning the covenant of our fathers? Judah has been faithless, and abomination has been committed in Israel and in Jerusalem; for Judah has profaned the sanctuary of the LORD, which He loves, and has married the daughter of a foreign god." The basic point in this message is: we all have one Father; one God has created us. In marriage both parties have to be, in the first place, children of one Father, faithful to the LORD their God, and for that reason, faithful to one another.

The LORD admonishes His people, saying that Judah has been faithless and that an abomination has been committed in Israel because they have married the daughter of a foreign god. Marriage should be part of the covenantal relationship with the LORD. Unfaithfulness in marriage is unfaithfulness to the LORD. That gives the married state a very special character. The apostle Paul calls the married state a profound mystery, referring to Christ and His Church (Ephesians 5:32). The relationship between Christ and His Church is set as an example for the relationship within holy wedlock. If we keep in mind this Biblical teaching, we will not speak lightly about separation and divorce. A marriage breakup is not just the partners' unfaithfulness to each other; it is unfaithfulness to the LORD and His covenant. That must make us very cautious in our approach to marriage breakup.

In Matthew 5:31,32, Jesus says: "It was also said, 'Whoever divorces his wife, let him give her a certificate of divorce.' But I say to you that everyone who divorces his wife, except on the ground of unchastity, makes her an adulteress: and whoever marries a divorced woman commits adultery." From this text it is clear that our Lord Jesus Christ disapproves of the way the certificate of divorce was used by the Jewish people.

We have seen already that the rule of Deuteronomy 24 did not "command" such a divorce, but that it was given to put restrictions on the use of an existing custom. In Jesus' time the death penalty for adultery had been abolished by the Roman government, and therefore the certificate of divorce was used also in cases of sexual unfaithfulness. The marriage then was terminated by the other party and therefore did not exist any longer. According to the Old Testament law, the other party would have been put to death. A divorce in such a case is legitimate. But in all other cases (Jesus says) they should work on reconciliation. When a man sends away his wife without a good reason, she may become the wife of someone else and in that way he would make her an adulteress. And the man who marries her who is divorced without good reason is also guilty of adultery.

This Scripture passage shows us that divorce is not allowed for all kinds of reasons, as was the custom with the Jewish people in Jesus' time. The only legitimate ground mentioned here for divorce is adultery in the legal sense, that is, one of the parties' sexual relations with someone outside the marriage. The marriage, consequently, has been dissolved and broken up by the unfaithfulness of the other party. In the Old Testament the guilty party was put to death and the other was "free." In the New Dispensation we do not use capital punishment in cases of sexual unfaithfulness, but it remains a reason for dissolving the marriage bond: the other party is free to remarry after the divorce.

There is still one more aspect I have to mention. Although adultery is a legitimate ground for divorce, there is no command to divorce. Deuteronomy forbids remarriage after a divorced wife has been married to another man. But the Bible never teaches us that the couple has to divorce after one has been unfaithful. It might even be preferable if they forgive and reconcile. The condition for such a reconciliation is, of course, that the unfaithful party gives up the extramarital relationship, repents, and makes a commitment to stay away from such practices in the future.

This repentance and amendment of life is an important factor also in another respect. Suppose that a wife has had a relationship with someone else and even expects a child from that relationship. Her husband has a legitimate right to request a divorce. He can send her away and is free from her. In the Old Testament she would have been put to death. The husband can marry another woman after his divorce, although he does not have to. He can agree to a reconciliation.

However, after he has been remarried, the possibility of reconciliation is eliminated. If the divorced woman, who was guilty of adultery, repents, amends her way of life, and asks for forgiveness of her sins, she cannot go back to her previous husband any longer. That is exactly what Deuteronomy 24 forbids. Then she is considered to be free as well. If she finds someone who is willing to marry her and take care of her and her child in a marriage "in the LORD," she may do so. The man who marries her does not commit adultery. In this situation, I do not believe that we can apply Matthew 5:32, where it says: "Whoever marries a divorced woman commits adultery." According to the context, our Lord Jesus Christ is speaking about a separation or a divorce on grounds other than adultery and about a man who marries a woman who is not legitimately free from her husband for that reason. However, in the situation we mentioned above the woman was an adulteress, but, before her repentance, the previous marriage had been definitively dissolved, and therefore, also the woman is no longer bound. It all depends on the question whether such a new marriage is a marriage "in the LORD," in obedience to His law and according to His covenantal relationship with His people.

7. The rules of I Corinthians 7

We have seen in the previous section that our Lord Jesus Christ in Matthew 5 and in Matthew 19 mentions only one legitimate reason for divorce. In I Corinthians 7 the apostle Paul mentions another reason. In verses 10-16 we read: "To the married I give charge, not I but the Lord, that the wife should not separate from the husband (but if she does, let her remain single or else be reconciled to her husband) - and that the husband should not divorce his wife. To the rest I say, not the Lord, that if any brother has a wife who is an unbeliever, and she consents to live with him, he should not divorce her. If any woman has a husband who is an unbeliever, and he consents to live with her, she should not divorce him. For the unbelieving husband is consecrated through his wife, and the unbelieving wife is consecrated through her husband. Otherwise your children would be unclean, but as it is they are holy. But if the unbelieving partner desires to separate, let it be so; in such a case the brother or sister is not bound. For God has called us to peace. Wife, how do you know whether you will save your husband? Husband, how do you know whether you will save your wife?"

In this Scripture portion we have to distinguish between two different cases, namely, in verses 10 and 11 and in verses 12—16. In verses 10 and 11 the apostle is apparently speaking to married couples where both husband and wife are members of the congregation. If there is something between them that disturbs their relationship as husband and wife, they should not break up their marriage. Here we find a reference to what we have learned from Matthew 5 and Matthew 19. He warns against the way the Jewish people abused the rule of Deuteronomy 24 to get divorce for all kinds of minor reasons. That he does not mention the exception of unchastity stands to reason, because his readers were well aware of the implications of such unfaithfulness. He warns them not to separate for all kinds of minor reasons but, even if it comes to a separation because of great difficulties and almost unbearable situations, to reconcile or to remain single. That is why separation (without divorce) has generally been accepted in the Christian church in cases of insurmountable difficulties between the two parties. As I stated before, such a separation can be a matter of: a. mutual agreement, perhaps for a certain period of time; b. a verdict of a judge on request of one of the parties in a situation of physical danger or; c. wilful desertion on the part of one against the will of the other.

In all these cases, as long as there is no unchastity involved, separation can be an outlet to prevent things from getting worse, but the aim should remain reconciliation, and neither of the parties is allowed to remarry. If they cannot reconcile, they should remain single.

In verses 12-16 the apostle mentions a completely new situation. If one of the two is a believer and the other is an unbeliever, the service of the Lord can become the main issue. We have to realize that the apostle here is by no means speaking about a believer who wants to get married to an unbeliever. That is something he clearly condemns in II Corinthians 6:14 ff.: "Do not be mismated with unbelievers. For what partnership have righteousness and iniquity? Or what fellowship has light with darkness? What accord has Christ with Belial? Or what has a believer in common with an unbeliever? What agreement has the temple of God with idols? For we are the temple of the living God."

In I Corinthians 7:12-16 the apostle refers to the situation where a couple got married while they were both unbelievers and later one of them became a Christian. That caused problems in the young congregation of Corinth. What were they supposed to do when their spouse did not want to serve the Lord? Their marriage could never become a marriage "in the LORD," within the covenantal relationship with their Father in heaven. In such a situation the apostle gives the advice to bear patiently with one another. He says: it has taken you quite a while to come to conversion. Through the grace of the Lord you have become a Christian, a believer, sanctified in Christ. Give your spouse time to consider these matters. Do not rush. You never know whether the Lord will work true conversion in your spouse's heart also. He might well use you and your Christian way of life as a testimony to convince him or her. If your spouse consents to live with you, do not divorce. However, there might come a time and a situation when he or she becomes a hindrance in your service of the Lord. If your spouse tries to make it impossible for you to serve the Lord, you have to obey God rather than man. Therefore, if the unbelieving partner desires to separate, let it be so. You have tried to save your marriage, but your choice to serve the Lord has brought your marriage to an end. "In such a case the brother or sister is not bound."

Here the apostle introduces a completely new situation. In the Old Testament this situation could not exist, because the position of the woman was of such a nature that she did not have a real choice. She simply had to obey and to follow her husband. Even if a Jewish man took a foreign wife, as was sometimes the case in times of war (when the girls were considered to belong to the "spoil of victory") then his wife had no choice but to participate in the worship service with her husband, regardless of whether she became a believer or not. The problem addressed by the apostle Paul in I Corinthians 7:12-16 became relevant in the early Christian churches, because the gospel was spread and the message of the Word of God was preached all over the world and each person individually, whether man or woman, had to make a personal choice: to believe and embrace the gospel or to reject the message. It is clear that when the apostle says in verse 15 "the brother or sister is not bound," he means that the marriage has been terminated. If the unbelieving partner persistently refuses to live together in peace and at least allow the other to serve the Lord without hindrance, then the believing partner is free. To me there is no doubt that this includes the possibility of a new marriage with a believer, a marriage "in the LORD."

8. Some conclusions

Bearing in mind what we have learned from Scripture in the foregoing sections, we will try to draw some practical conclusions for situations which we have to face today in our society and among Christians.

Our starting point and norm has to be that a marriage, according to the Word of God, is terminated and finished only through the death of one of the partners. What God has joined together let not man put asunder. If there are problems in the relationship between husband and wife, even almost insurmountable obstacles, they should always try to reconcile. However, a separation, perhaps for a shorter or longer period of time, may be the only remedy to prevent things from getting worse and to avoid even physical harm. Such a separation, however, does not mean a divorce. The aim and target should remain reconciliation.

A divorce, with the possibility of remarriage, should only be considered in two cases. Either when one of the parties is guilty of unchastity, or when one of the partners is an unbeliever and makes it impossible for the other to serve the Lord. In both situations a divorce with the option of remarriage is legitimate, although not necessary. If someone prefers to leave open the possibility of reconciliation, he or she does not have to divorce. A separation may suffice.

Although divorce should not take place for any other reason than we have mentioned above, we have to face the reality that it still happens. If, without the consent of the believing partner, a divorce has resulted and the other partner either has become guilty of fornication or has married someone else, the divorced partner is free to remarry. He or she does not commit adultery, because their marriage has been definitively dissolved by the other party.

If a divorce has taken place because of one of the partners' unchastity, the innocent partner is allowed to remarry. If after such a remarriage the guilty party comes to repentance and amendment of life, there is no possibility to reconcile anymore. Then also the other party is free to remarry "in the LORD" with a believer who is prepared to accept the past. This might be very important for a young woman who has been divorced and has to take care of a child born out of unchastity. The man who marries her does not commit adultery.

The Westminster Confession and a great number of theologians consider a divorce and subsequent remarriage also legitimate in cases of "such wilful desertion as can in no way be remedied by the church or civil magistrate." I doubt whether that is correct. What is "wilful desertion as can in no way be remedied?" To me it is too vague. I can see that the relationship can be disturbed and disrupted in such a way that it seems to be irreparable. A continuation of the relationship can become an almost unbearable ordeal. In such a situation a separation may be necessary and unavoidable. Still I am not convinced that there is a legitimate basis for a divorce on Biblical grounds, as long as there is no unchastity or the situation described in I Corinthians 7. That means: both parties should remain single, hoping and praying for reconciliation. What the LORD has joined together man shall not put asunder. I cannot see that "wilful desertion" is a Biblical ground for divorce and remarriage. Instead, it opens the door for the same abuse that the Jewish people made of the certificate of divorce, mentioned in Deuteronomy 24 and condemned by Jesus in Matthew 19.

9. Discipline

Some remarks must be made with respect to church discipline in all such situations.

Earlier I mentioned already that the word *adultery* can be used in different ways. The original meaning of the word was: to mix the real and pure thing with something of inferior quality, like mixing wine with water. In contemporary English the word *adultery* means: a sexual relationship of a married person with someone who is not his or her spouse. The Bible and the Heidelberg Catechism in Lord's Day 41 use the word *adultery* in a much broader sense, namely, for everything that disrupts the married state or that defiles body or soul, which have to be kept pure and holy as temples of the Holy Spirit.

Therefore, sin against the seventh commandment and the discipline of the church in such cases is much more comprehensive than what the world calls *adultery*.

Further we must consider that discipline always involves a sinner who is not willing to amend his or her life and who continues in sin. That might have consequences in cases of divorce as well.

When someone comes to a divorce or even a remarriage which is not acceptable according to the Word of God, the office-bearers must speak up and admonish. However, when the sinner acknowledges that what he did was not right, and repents, the results of such wrongdoing cannot always be undone. A single woman should not become pregnant, but unwed mothers do exist. When divorce has occurred and the brother or sister has married someone else, there is no going back to the way it was. That is exactly what Deuteronomy 24 forbids. Admonition must take place and after repentance has been shown and confession of sin has taken place before the office-bearers, discipline has come to an end.

We must always be aware of the danger of people acting in a hypocritical way; for example, when someone goes a certain route knowing that as soon as the marriage has become a *fait accompli* he can simply "confess" his mistake while still achieving what he wanted in the first place. However, that can happen also in other instances; for example, when someone makes public profession of faith or joins the church just to get married. We must judge what is in the heart of man by the testimony they give and by the clear evidence of that testimony in their way of life. Only the Lord can see what is truly in man's heart and He will be the ultimate judge.

10. Final remarks

I have mentioned Deuteronomy 24 and Matthew 19 a number of times. With respect to Deuteronomy 24 one remark has to be made. We read about an "indecency" which might be a ground for divorce. We have seen that unchastity or extramarital relations are legitimate grounds for divorce. There are, however, some other possible cases to which Deuteronomy 24 may refer as well. Physical infirmities or other things which make a real married life impossible, and which are purposely hidden from the other party until the day of the wedding, may, in some cases, constitute a ground for divorce or, rather, may bring one face-to-face with the reality that the marriage vows were not valid but were a matter of deception. Although very rare, it does happen that someone finds out after the wedding that the partner is a homosexual or, for another reason, is not willing or able to establish a sexual relationship, while this was purposely hidden from the other until the day of the wedding. Of course, marriage is much more than a sexual relationship, and a marriage in which husband and wife are a real "help fit for him or her" is quite well possible even without sexual relations. Many cases prove this reality. However, the sexual relationship is certainly an integral part of it. If one of the partners purposely keeps secret the impossibility of such relations, it can be a ground to dissolve the marriage. We should then not speak about a *divorce* but about a so-called *matrimonium non consummatum:* a marriage which was not consummated or never became a reality. Even the Roman Catholic Church, which is very strict about divorce, recognizes such a case. It is basically a matter of deception rather than of faithfulness.

Finally, we have seen that divorce should not exist, but as long as sin, and the devastating influence of it, has not been taken away, we will be confronted with mankind's hardness of heart. That was already so in the Old Testament, as we have learned from Deuteronomy 24. It will remain so until our Lord Jesus Christ returns on the clouds of heaven. Then there will be no divorce any longer. There will not even be marriage any longer — only the great marriage feast of the Lamb.

Let us as Christians, live together in the married state, in a way that is in accordance with what the apostle Paul says in Ephesians 5:25-32: "Husbands, love your wives, as Christ loves the church and gave Himself up for her, that He might sanctify her, having cleansed her by the washing of water with the Word, that He might present the church to Himself in splendour, without spot or wrinkle or any such thing, that she might be holy and without blemish. Even so husbands should love their wives as their own bodies. He who loves his wife loves himself. For no man ever hates his own flesh, but nourishes and cherishes it, as Christ does the church, because we are members of His body. 'For this reason a man shall leave his father and mother and be joined to his wife, and the two shall become one flesh.' This mystery is a profound one, and I am saying that it refers to Christ and the church."

We can count on our God of the covenant and on our Lord Jesus Christ. He will never divorce the Bride He has chosen and prepared for Himself — His Church — the church of which we are allowed to be members, by mere grace.

CHAPTER THREE

Marriage and Procreation

1. What is at stake?

This is the third chapter dealing with a marriage-related issue. The first chapter deals specifically with preparation for the married state: the young people work on getting better acquainted with one another before they enter into the holy married state. In the second chapter we pay attention to a completely different matter: not every married couple lives happily ever after, not even those who seriously try to maintain peace and harmony in the married state; divorce and separation take place also among believers. In this chapter we will deal with the relationship between marriage and having children. In the old Form for the Solemnization of Marriage it says: "that by marriage the human race is to be propagated." In Genesis 1:28 we read about the divine promise and blessing which the LORD gave to Adam and Eve. This promise and blessing was also an instruction: "Be fruitful and multiply and fill the earth and subdue it; and have dominion over the fish of the sea and over the birds of the air and over every living thing that moves upon the earth." This shows us clearly the relationship between marriage and having children.

There are a number of rather formal expressions which I will use quite frequently in this chapter, although they may not be very common to every reader. To ensure that everyone understands the meaning of these expressions, I will first provide you with some definitions.

Intercourse, in general, means an exchange of feelings or actions which make people know each other more closely. In the context of this chapter it refers to the act of sexual unity in which husband and wife become "one flesh." This word can be used also for a mere social contact. Therefore we refer to it as sexual intercourse, in distinction from social intercourse.

Procreation is the act of producing or bringing forth offspring. The word *propagation,* used in the old Form for the Solemnization of Marriage has a slightly different meaning. With *propagation* the emphasis is on the increase of the number of descendants by bringing forth new life, while *procreation* refers to the bringing forth of offspring per se.

Conception is the beginning of new life by the union of a male and a female cell.

From these definitions it is clear that we can only speak about procreation, if intercourse is followed by conception.

Abstinence, in general, means staying away from pleasant things, such as drinking alcohol. In the context of this chapter it means to abstain from sexual intercourse.

After the publication of an article about marriage and divorce, I received a number of requests to deal also with the relationship between marriage and procreation. That is a very current and controversial issue today. Even among believers there is no unanimity in this respect. In the world we can hear the statement: "We first want to enjoy life; we want to be free, not tied down right away with kids. We first want to be married for a while, to get to know each other better, to save some money, and to finish our studies, and then, probably, we will 'have' one or two kids."

There are many who do not consider the married state necessary for having children. They voluntarily and deliberately chose for a life as a single parent. However, for us as Christians it should be perfectly clear that marriage and procreation are inseparably connected. Although single parents exist, they are (and should be) exceptions. Such a state can be caused by the death of one of the parents, by a marriage break-up, or by an out-of-wedlock pregnancy. In all these cases we are dealing with the existing reality, but at the same time with a clear exception.

There are also childless marriages. A marriage without children can still be a meaningful marriage and fruitful in the service of the Lord. Nevertheless, it is an exception, no matter what the reason may be. I am not sure whether people always see it this way. In fact, I am afraid that young couples too often consider it quite normal and legitimate to "wait" a number of years before they "have" a child. Some want to finish their studies, others want to save money to buy a house or simply to enjoy life and freedom, before they take on the responsibility of raising children. Others consider themselves not "mature enough" and postpone the responsibility for a growing family for that reason. Couples who already have one or two children wonder whether it is "time" to have another one.

The main point is: When and to what extent is there an obligation, a "command," to procreate, to bring forth children. Are we supposed to bring forth the maximum number of children? Some speak about the "optimum" number and see that as the responsibility and ability, not only to bring forth, but also to raise, to instruct, and to bring to maturity, the children which are entrusted to them. The maximum number may not always coincide with the ability to bring them all up in a responsible way.

When we consider all these things, it is understandable that the request was made to deal also with these aspects of married life. If certain restrictions are necessary, the question arises: How and in what way are we supposed to "regulate" the number of children and the interval between the births of the children? What criteria are we supposed to apply? What measures are we supposed to take? What is legitimate and what is not?

In response to some reactions and questions which I received, I will try to deal with the matters just mentioned. I consider it very important that these things are openly discussed. The most dangerous situation is always when an existing problem is denied or ignored, because then everyone tries to find his or her own answer, without the help and support which we can give each other in an open and honest discussion. The chance that someone goes the wrong way is much greater if we avoid discussing these things than if we try to help each other in these, certainly very delicate, matters.

2. A changing attitude

Also among Christians, the attitude regarding the number of children to have is changing. Half a century ago the general point of view was that any limitation of the number of children in a Christian family was in conflict with the Word of God. The number of children was something we had to leave in the hands of the Lord. Only if the mother was seriously ill and in a life-threatening situation, was a couple allowed to abstain from procreation, but then the only acceptable method was total abstinence. Although the economic circumstances then were much worse than today, most families were much larger than in our modern times. It is an undeniable fact that, if all Christian couples would live according to the old rules, there would still be families with twelve or even twenty children, as it sometimes happened in the past. I am not judging in any individual case. A marriage can remain childless for many reasons, and the number of children can remain one or two even when the parents would like to have, and do everything "they can," to receive more children. However, it is a fact that the average size of families is much smaller than in the past, also among Christians.

The reason why this is so is that people deliberately take certain measures to limit the number of children. If that were not so, the average size of families would be even *larger* than in the past. Through better medical care there are fewer stillborn babies and miscarriages than in the past, and the number of children who die before they reach the age of one year is much smaller than half a century ago. That means that the same number of conceptions results in at least twice the number of healthy children. And yet, the family size is decreasing.

We all agree, or at least are supposed to acknowledge, that according to the Word of God sexual intercourse is only allowed within the marriage state. However, not everyone thinks the same way about the relationship between intercourse and having children. A minister, by virtue of his office, is sometimes confronted with marriage problems and is supposed to "counsel" people in such a situation. Once a mother complained: "I do not understand why my husband wants to have intercourse while I am already pregnant? The only reason should be to procreate a child and that has taken place already!" This mother saw the sexual act only as a necessary means to receive a child and had no idea what the true sexual relation between husband and wife is all about.

Although it may sound strange to some, such situations still exist, more than we are aware of. However, today most Christians agree that, although the sexual relationship has to be restricted to the married state, the sexual act is not only for purposes of procreation. The very fact that conception is impossible in a certain situation, does not make intercourse meaningless. It is a gift of the Lord, a way in which a husband and wife can experience the most intimate relationship of love and unity. The Lord has connected this act with the bringing forth of children, but it certainly has its own value, also without the direct intention or result of bringing forth a child. If a couple knows that, because of physical aberrations, it is impossible to receive a child, that does not make their sexual life senseless. It still is a gift of the LORD given to them in the married state.

However, the question remains: In how far, when, how, and for what reasons are parents allowed to take measures to avoid or postpone the conception of another child?

3. Valid reasons

The most frequently used reason for limiting the number of children (so-called family planning) is the danger of overpopulation. Not enough food will be available. Poverty and starvation will be the final result. However, is that really an honest reason? It is a well-known fact that family planning always has been an issue, especially among well-to-do families. Those who financially could well afford to have a large family were often the least willing to accept this responsibility. Family size is often greater in poor countries than in wealthy areas. Overpopulation and starvation is not a real threat for the people who are the most in favour of having a small family. We can understand that the food supply is a problem in some parts of the world, but those are the places with the largest families. That is not the problem in rich countries.

Overpopulation does not exist in our part of the world. On the contrary. In many developed countries there is a problem in the opposite direction. Sociologists have figured out that after some years, there will be a large number of people to look after, with only a relatively small group of people to take care of them. In some countries the government is considering measures to reverse this effect by encouraging people to have a larger family, because they are concerned about the decreasing population.

The real reason for the smaller families is that people do not like the responsibility. They want to be free, to enjoy life without being hindered too much by the raising of children. They want to have fun, to have sexual relations, but they do not want children. And when a girl gets pregnant, she wants to have the right to get rid of the baby by abortion. "Don't care about others, just live for your own joy and have as much fun as possible." That is the mentality today.

Are there, then, no valid reasons at all to restrict the number of children or to postpone a pregnancy within the scope of our own responsibility? There certainly are. The LORD did not give mankind the instruction to multiply as much and as fast as possible; He said to Adam and Eve that they should be fruitfull and multiply, and fill the earth and *subdue* it, and have *dominion* over everything on the earth. Parents have the responsibility, not only to bring forth children, but to bring them up in the fear of the Lord. As many children as possible is not necessarily in accordance with the commandments of the LORD. It is irresponsible to procreate another child if, humanly speaking, the parents know that the life or the health of the mother will be in danger, or that the upbringing of the existing family will become very difficult, if not impossible. Many circumstances have to be considered and it is impossible to set a clear-cut rule for every situation. It makes quite a difference whether a family lives in a small apartment, because the father is unemployed and the mother cannot make ends meet, or that a family lives in a huge farmhouse, and the children work on the family farm. Parents have to consider all aspects. Prayerfully they have to bring this matter before the Lord. They can discuss it with their pastor, with their doctor, with one of the elders, or with another "counselor," but finally *they* have to make the decision before the countenance of the Lord.

It is certainly not so that a mother should become pregnant as soon as possible after she has given birth to a baby. Let us not forget that in our present situation the chance that a mother gets pregnant again within a year is much greater than it was, for instance, in the time of the Old Testament. In the Bible we read on different occasions that a child was weaned. For instance, in Genesis 21:8 it says about Isaac: "And the child grew, and was weaned; and Abraham made a great feast on the day that Isaac was weaned." In I Samuel 1:23,24, we read about Hannah, the mother of the prophet Samuel: "The woman remained and nursed her son, until she weaned him. And when she had weaned him, she took him up with her, along with a three-year-old bull, and an ephah of flour, and a skin of wine; and she brought him to the house of the LORD at Shiloh; and the child was *young*." In both cases, with Isaac as well as with Samuel, it is very likely that the boys were about five years old before they were "weaned." Do you realize what that means? A mother was supposed to breastfeed her baby for a number of years. Often three to five years. During that period of time it was very unlikely that she would become pregnant again. That was a "natural" reason why two children were seldom born within a year. There were at least a number of years in between. The question is not whether there can be circumstances which make it advisable or necessary to refrain from the procreation of another child, but the question is *what* the proper *reasons* are and *what* measures have to be taken to prevent or avoid a pregnancy for a certain period of time.

4. Different circumstances

What measures have to be taken and are appropriate in a certain situation depends on the personal circumstances and the "weight" of the reasons. When the mother is healthy, and nurses the baby herself for about a year, no special measures may be necessary. If there is some concern about the health of the mother and about the way she will be able to take care of a growing family, a certain period of abstinence and self-control may be in place.

If there are more pressing reasons, other measures may have to be considered. What measures have to be taken depends on the circumstances. That applies in two directions. If a couple has been married for half a year and there is still no pregnancy, there is no reason to be alarmed. However, if after a couple of years there still is no baby, the couple could see a doctor and ask for some tests to find out whether there is a specific reason for infertility. After they have been married for more than ten years they may consider a rather complicated operation in an effort to cure the problem. Let us not forget that this is also a human effort to intervene in "nature," in the same way as every visit to the doctor's office is an attempt to use the means available to control a situation, as far as we can. We are allowed to use the means the Lord has made available, as long as we do it in a responsible way. A treatment is not right or wrong per se, but we can use anything in a wrong way.

The same applies to methods to regulate or delay pregnancy. They always must be in accordance with the circumstances and in accordance with the responsibility the Lord has given us. If, in a certain situation, a pregnancy, according to medical indications, would be fatal, it is irresponsible to cause such a pregnancy. Of course, we can never say whether it will really be fatal, but we have to go by what we know, to the best of our ability. If you know that you have heart disease, and your doctor gives you a warning to avoid certain things, then you should not take the risk of causing a heart attack. It is the same with a pregnancy. In such a situation strict measures have to be taken. This is a very delicate matter and we should not think too lightly about it or be too hasty in judging people without knowing all the circumstances. Practice has proven that this can be a very difficult decision for the parents concerned and that they are sometimes hurt by inconsiderate remarks from outsiders who do not understand the problems they have to deal with.

It is a fact that such situations do not occur very often, although it may happen more than most people are aware of. In most cases the reasons are not so dramatic and the postponement of a pregnancy is less urgent. Then less drastic measures are in place. Periodical abstinence or the "rhythm method" of birth control may be the proper way to deal with the matter. This method of regulating or postponing pregnancy is even accepted in the Roman Catholic Church and is the only permissible way, according the the Papal Encyclical Letter, "Humanae Vitae." With this method, parents take into consideration the fact that the mother is fertile only during a restricted number of days before and after ovulation. If abstinence is exercised during those days, a pregnancy can be avoided or postponed. If this method is used under medical supervision and with the help of temperature registration, it is a reliable method. It does not give complete certainty, but in most situations that is not necessary either. As a method for some "regulation" it may be sufficient. It has already been mentioned that there can be situations in which a pregnancy should be avoided under all circumstances. Then this method may not be applicable. However, in most cases the situation is not so serious.

Basically the question *of what* method can be used is a matter of secondary importance. The main question is whether there are *valid reasons* to postpone or avoid pregnancy in the first place. If this point has been discussed and satisfactorily answered in prayer before the countenance of the Lord, then the question what method is appropriate can be discussed with a doctor, provided that he is prepared to consider the Biblical norms. Because not everyone is in a position to discuss such questions with a physician who understands his or her feelings, it may be worthwhile to say a few more things about this delicate matter.

5. Abstinence

In the past total abstinence was seen as the only alternative when pregnancy had to be avoided. This was more or less a result of the Roman Catholic attitude towards sexual life and abstinence. This point of view becomes particularly clear in celibacy. A Roman Catholic priest is not allowed to marry but must abstain from any sexual relationship his whole life long. They often refer to Paul who was also unmarried. He writes in I Corinthians 7:32-35: "The unmarried man is anxious about the affairs of the Lord, how to please the Lord; but the married man is anxious about worldly affairs, how to please his wife, and his interests are divided. And the unmarried woman or girl is anxious about the affairs of the Lord, how to be holy in body and spirit; but the married woman is anxious about worldly affairs, how to please her husband. I say this for your benefit, not to lay a restraint upon you, but to promote good order and to secure your undivided devotion to the Lord."

If this text is used to make abstinence mandatory for everyone who preaches the gospel and who wants to serve the Lord with his whole life in a special way, it is taken out of context. The apostle Paul also says that not everyone has the "gift" of continence. In I Corinthians 7:7 and 9 he writes in this respect: "Each has his special gift from God, one of one kind and one of another . . . . If they cannot exercise self-control, they should marry. For it is better to marry than to be aflame with passion." The apostle does not say that sexual life is something to be ashamed of or something which cannot go together with the service of the Lord. Paul's situation was special; he had to fulfil a unique mandate. He speaks in I Corinthians 7:26 about "the present distress" in which they "will have worldly troubles." Overemphasis of the unmarried state has led to a wrong idea about sexual life.

In the past sexual intercourse was considered to be almost indecent. It was necessary to bring forth children but, apart from that, it was a carnal matter and could not really go together with spiritual things. It was never openly discussed. Nowadays things are quite different, almost to the other extreme. There seem to be no "secrets" at all; sexual matters are discussed very openly, but unfortunately not always respectfully. Sex has come out into the open and, in the opinion of many, is not inseparably connected with the married state any longer. There seem to be no norms at all. Rather, mankind has become its own norm. What makes you feel good is what is good, as long as it does not hurt anyone else.

The result of this attitude in the past was that total abstinence was seen as the only acceptable method to use when a pregnancy was not desirable. Every other solution was considered immoral and unnatural. However, it was a rather hypocritical attitude. Theory and reality where often miles apart. Besides, it was a denial of the wonderful gift of unity which the LORD had given within the holy married state. Sexual intercourse is certainly not a "carnal" matter; it is not an indecent act. It is a gift of the LORD, given already in paradise. The LORD uses this act to bring forth new life. But also when the procreation of new life is not the intention or cannot even be expected, it remains a very important part of marriage and a way in which husband and wife express their feeling of love and unity. In Ephesians 5:31,32, the apostle Paul says: "For this reason a man shall leave his father and mother and be joined to his wife, and the two shall become one flesh. This mystery is a profound one, and I am saying that it refers to Christ and the church." The unity of husband and wife in the married state is used as a symbol of the relationship between Christ and His Church and it is called a profound mystery. In the same way a caricature of this relationship is used as a symbol of sin and the work of Satan. In the Book of Revelation the dominion of the devil and his activity is compared with a harlot (Revelation 17:1 and 19:2). In the Old Testament unfaithfulness to the LORD is often called "spiritual adultery." In Jeremiah 3:6 the LORD admonishes His people and says that they "have played the harlot" by serving other gods.

Is total abstinence the only acceptable alternative when pregnancy has to be avoided? Although other methods are called "unnatural," the question has to be asked whether it is "natural" when a husband and wife live together, sharing everything in life, without having the opportunity to come to a very essential act in the married state. Isn't that an unnatural and unhealthy situation? Of course, self-control is important and to abstain from sexual intercourse for a certain period of time can even strengthen the bond of marriage. In I Corinthians 7:5 the apostle says: "Do not refuse one another except perhaps by agreement for a season, that you may devote yourselves to prayer; but then come together again, lest Satan tempt you through lack of self-control." Here he speaks about abstinence for a specific reason, with mutual agreement. And he adds: but then come together again, "lest Satan tempt you." If a couple permanently has to live in total abstinence, it will have its impact on the relationship. The consequence can be that they cannot share the same bedroom any longer. Let us be realistic. We would not allow a boy and a girl who are engaged to live together in the same house and certainly not to sleep together in the same room. Even if they would say that they are strong enough to withstand the temptation, it would be irresponsible to permit it. It would cause unbearable tension. By the same token it is almost impossible to expect a young couple, with normal sexual feelings and reactions, to live together without having sexual intercourse. It would bring them into an extremely difficult position and place enormous stress on them. No one can, in all honesty, call this a "natural" situation.

Today we live in a society in which sex seems to be the most important thing in life. That is a caricature and to a certain extent idolatry with the body. We utterly reject this worldly attitude. But we should not, as a reaction, go to the other extreme and consider sexual intercourse unimportant and indecent. It is given as one of the most wonderful ways of expressing the unity within the holy married state. It has to be reserved for the married state and restricted to the relationship between husband and wife, but, used and seen in the proper context, it is a gift of the LORD which we should not underestimate or debase.

6. Other acceptable methods

We have seen that there *are* situations in which a pregnancy has to be avoided or postponed, and that there are even situation in which causing a new pregnancy would be irresponsible. We have acknowledged that *total abstinence* is not the ideal and natural way out. We therefore have to consider what other options are possible. The main point has to be, as we noted before, that the couple, in all honesty before the Lord, has considered their task and mandate and has come to the conclusion that they have to avoid a pregnancy within the scope of their own responsibility. It is important to *repeat* this, because our heart is "deceitful above all things, and desperately corrupt; who can understand it?" (Jeremiah 17:9). We are all prone by nature to go the way of least resistance and to seek our own pleasure, rather than being concerned about the commandments of the Lord.

One of the most commonly used methods is the "pill." Are Christians allowed to use this? Let us first state that the pill has to be seen as a medicine, prescribed by a physician. The use of this or any other medicines without the supervision and advice of a doctor is dangerous. There are many rumors about known as well as unknown side effects. We have to be careful with these stories. For someone who is not a doctor it is very difficult to draw conclusions. Every medicine has known side effects and there is always a risk of unknown side effects. Therefore the advice and supervision of a doctor is necessary. But, provided that there are valid reasons for postponing a pregnancy and provided that proper consultation with a doctor has taken place, I cannot see that the use of this medicine has to be condemned in all circumstances. Besides, this "pill" was originally not developed to avoid pregnancy but rather to cure infertility. After using this medicine for a certain period of time, the chance of pregnancy increases. That is the way it was originally used and it is still used that way in many instances. However, this same medicine can also be used to avoid pregnancy for a certain period of time.

There are situations in which this method can be used also by Christians. Some say: "It is unnatural; it intrudes into the secret works of the Lord, which are beautifully described in Psalm 139." However, is not every use of medicines a matter of intervening in a "natural" process? Still we accept a doctor's prescription in most cases. A Caesarean section is not a "natural" process either, but is nevertheless acceptable.

Another argument is that medicines should be given only to people who are sick, and that in these situations there is often not a trace of sickness. However, there are many circumstances in which we use medicines, although not ill, only to avoid certain unpleasant things which *might* happen. Many people ask the doctor for a "shot" to avoid a possible bout of flu in the winter season. Vaccinations and all kinds of prophylactic medicines are administered regularly, and usually there is no trace of illness. Let us not forget that total abstinence can create great psychological tension and put the relationship between the partners in jeopardy. It can do harm to the whole family. If one of the partners cannot carry the burden any longer, he or she may end up going to the doctor to get a "tranquilizer." It would be more "natural" to avoid such tensions by using a contraceptive medicine than to take medicines to cope with the stress caused by total abstinence.

There is one more remark I would like to make in this respect. It is impossible to mention all available methods. Which method to use is a matter which has to be discussed with a doctor and has to be decided on medical grounds, after the principle decision has been made by the parents on Biblical grounds. However, there are methods which are unacceptable under *all* circumstances and those are the abortive means. When I say *abortive*, I am referring not only to an abortion, as performed today in many hospitals and abortion clinics, but also to methods which do not *prevent* conception but which *destroy* already-present human life. To these abortive methods belong the "morning-after" pill as well as IUDs. An IUD is a device inserted in the uterus to prevent a fertilized ovum from imbedding in the uterus. These methods are unacceptable because they basically cause a small-scale abortion: they kill the beginning of human life.

7. A childless marriage

There is still one aspect I would like to touch on, and that is a very important one for many a young family. We hear quite often about couples who decide to get married but who wait a number of years before they "start a family." Many reasons are mentioned. Some want to finish their studies; others want to save some money or buy a house; others first want to get to know each other better before taking on the responsibility of raising children. In The Netherlands, in the Reformed press, there was a public discussion about this matter. The main point in this discussion was the position of students who do not have a job or the means to provide for a family, but who do not want to prolong their engagement. Many years of engagement, they say, make it almost impossible to live a "chaste and disciplined life." Therefore they would rather live together legitimately in marriage, and wait with having children until they can afford it. This reasoning sounds sincere and it seems to make sense. They do not want to separate sexual unity from the married state. They say they prefer this to the hypocritical way of those who use the pill while they are only engaged.

It is certainly true that those who marry without accepting the responsibility for raising a family are more honest and less hypocritical than those who live together without being married. However, that does not make it right. We have to remember that the LORD gave mankind the instruction, within the holy married state: "Be fruitful and multiply, and fill the earth and subdue it." The LORD laid the connection between marriage and having children. There can be valid reasons to delay the birth of another child. We have to consider the circumstances carefully. Not all cases are the same. But we should not separate what the LORD has joined together. If a couple is not yet ready to begin a family because they have no house, no money to provide for a family, or are not mature enough for it, they should not marry. It is not correct to want the privileges of the married state, without accepting the responsibilities that go with it. What the LORD has joined together man should not put asunder. The situation is quite different with parents who are married, who have accepted the responsibilities, but who for one reason or another have to "regulate" the size or the rate of growth of their family. The sexual relationship between husband and wife is a beautiful gift of the LORD which can be enjoyed within the holy married state, also when the procreation of children is not the primary intention. But we should not *separate* the two and try to *grasp* the one without *accepting* the other.

I realize that these matters are not easy to deal with. They are very delicate. Everyone may not agree with what has been said in this chapter. However, I hope that I have given some food for thought and some guidelines in a matter which many have questions about, but which is not discussed enough in a Christian way, to each other's upbuilding.

CHAPTER FOUR

The Unmarried State

1. Full-fledged members

In the previous chapters we have dealt with different aspects of marriage. We have paid attention to the way people get to know each other and enter into the married state. We have also looked at the other side of the coin. Not every couple lives happily ever after. Divorce takes place. In a third chapter we discussed some aspects of a growing family and the parents' responsibility with respect to the size of their family.

The content of these chapters is partially in response to practical questions raised by readers, as well as the result of cases dealt with in my experience as a pastor. I do not mention any specific cases in a recognizable way, nor do I refer to persons in such a way that they can be identified by the readers, although many statements are based on experience and some readers may feel that their personal questions are being dealt with and answered.

Also this chapter is initiated by specific questions raised by readers and is partially based on experience.

I will pay special attention to the position of brothers and sisters who never get married. What is their place in our community, especially within the communion of saints? Do they have a legitimate, fully accepted place, or are they treated as special cases? Are they, to a certain extent, incomplete members? Are they weird and exceptional persons with whom you cannot even discuss the problems of everyday (family) life? Are they to be treated with pity because they are so lonely, or are they to be envied because they have such an easy life, not having the cares and concerns of a family? It is a fact that they often are treated and feel treated that way, instead of being accepted as full-fledged members of the church.

Sometimes an unmarried man is not considered eligible for the office of elder or deacon because the apostle Paul says (in I Timothy 3:4) that an office-bearer "must manage his own house well, keeping his children submissive and respectful in every way"; and (in verse 2) that a deacon "must be the husband of one wife." That, of course, is a wrong exegesis of this text, because the condition, "the husband of one wife," in this respect does not mean a minimum, but a maximum. It means: not two or more wives, as frequently happened in those days, but only one. And the condition "keeping his children submissive" does not mean that someone who has no children should be excluded for that reason. We all know that there are ministers who remain single. One of the most prominent apostles, Paul himself, was unmarried.

The basic point is that all members of the congregation have their own specific task, mandate, and responsibility. They all have their own capacities and restrictions, their own gifts and talents, no matter whether they are single or married, whether they have a large family or no children at all. The most important thing is that everyone must use his or her talents and gifts readily and cheerfully in the service of the Lord, to His glory and for the benefit and well-being of other members. (See Heidelberg Catechism Lord's Day 21, answer 55.)

Based on this principle, we will have a closer look at the position of unmarried members in the congregation.

2. Why unmarried?

A variety of reasons can be adduced as to why a person remains unmarried, and often it is a combination of reasons that cannot always be clearly determined.

Most boys and girls get engaged before they are twenty and get married between the ages of twenty and twenty-five. That is the ordinary course of events. Past that age it is more difficult to find a partner for life. Why? For a variety of reasons. Younger people are more spontaneous in seeking and establishing a relationship. At a younger age there are more potential partners "available." Because most young people have made their choice before they are twenty, after twenty-five there are not many "left." Besides, those who are still single at that age are sometimes considered somewhat odd. That makes it even more difficult.

Still, there can be all kinds of respectable reasons why someone remains single for many years. It is not always a matter of not (yet) being interested in a lasting relationship, although that may be the reason in some cases. It can be a matter of being too critical at first, and refusing some "chances," hoping for a more desirable partner, with the result that one finally is left without a lasting friendship. However, we as Christians have to see the hand of the Lord in bringing together husband and wife. That is what the Form for the Solemnization of Marriage says and that is what we confess as a reality. That does not take away our own responsibility, however. The Lord brings together, but He wants us to work and to accept our own task and responsibility. No one should just sit idle, waiting for the Lord to "bring" a partner to him, in the meantime complaining that there still is no one. To pray and to work is an instruction which counts for every area of human life, including finding a marriage partner. In the same way, just as someone who is engaged with an unbeliever should not blame the Lord for "bringing them together," so someone who sits idle and waits should not complain that the Lord did not "bring" him or her a partner.

Another factor can be that the person lives in a small congregation and has little choice. We all agree (at least we should recognize the fact) that a marriage has to be based on the unity of faith in the Lord and that no partner should be sought outside the church. The apostle Paul says in II Corinthians 6:14: "Do not be mismated with unbelievers." However, the inevitable consequence is that people in a small congregation have little choice and little opportunity to find a friend. Let us not ignore or overlook this part of the problem, and let us try to help them in this respect as much as we can, for instance, by organizing, in an appropriate way, regular contacts between young members of our congregations.

A final reason I would like to mention is that some are very disappointed in contacts they have had with members of the church. Too often we hear young people complain about the moral standards they were confronted with on their first date and who are turned off by such an attitude. Also in this respect there is lots of work to be done by the parents in keeping an eye on the attitudes and moral standards developed and applied by their children. A lack of communication in this respect can cause lasting damage and a way of life which is contrary to the Word of God. Ignoring or denying this reality only makes things worse.

3. The position of unmarried members

How do we treat unmarried members? That is an important question! Too many unmarried people are hurt because they are dealt with in a wrong way. It does not always happen on purpose. Most of the harm done is unintentional. No one likes to be singled out or to be treated as an exception. We do not know why a certain person never got married, nor do we know why a couple has no children. In general, it is none of our business, as long as the people concerned do not talk about it themselves. During a homevisit it can be brought up, but in general we should show discretion and not curiously interfere in these matters. But we do have to treat these people as full-fledged members of the church. That may sound obvious, but it is not so generally practised. I would like to relate a number of rather unpleasant experiences which can be avoided if we are a little more thoughtful about the position of our fellow members.

Sometimes certain jobs are assigned to single persons because they have lots of time on their hands anyway. That may be true in some cases, but as a rule unmarried people have their own way of life and are not less busy than other people. They do not have to worry about certain things, but they have other things which are not so obvious to people who have a family. We should respect them in the same way as we do others and leave how they spend their time and set their priorities up to them. They should share in the work in the congregation in the *same* way as all other members. Not more and not less.

We also have to watch the way we talk about our brothers and sisters. It hurts when single persons hear remarks about their holiday trip like: "They can easily go wherever they want, because they have neither chick nor child." It may be true that single people can spend more money on a holiday trip than parents who have a large family, but lots of them would rather be surrounded by their own family, if they had one, than to spend their time with strangers in a more expensive holiday resort. Another thing is the private lives of these members. They are frequently asked to come over for a visit, to drop in, or to babysit, but they do not receive much company. It is nice to be invited to come over to someone's place and to be welcomed as guest, but they often feel sad that they are always a guest and never a host or hostess, and that they depend on others and have little privacy. It would be very much appreciated if we visited the single members more often. That counts for those who are unmarried as well as for those who are widowed.

The next point of consideration is our conversations. When married people are together, especially married women, they often talk about their children and the raising of children. Two aspects have to be kept in mind in this respect, in order not to hurt the feelings of others unnecessarily. In the first place, we have to acknowledge that single persons as well as people who have no children, although they have no personal experience in raising their own children, certainly can have an opinion which is worth considering. An "outsider" can sometimes judge more objectively than someone who is fully involved in a matter. It hurts, it is unreasonable, and it is not a Christian attitude, if we let them feel in one way or another that their opinion is of no value. Remarks like: "What do you know about it?" or "That is easy for you to say, because you have no children," are out of order. Let us treat our brothers and sisters in a fair and respectful way, and avoid hurting others unnecessarily.

In the second place we have to be careful that we do not avoid certain issues because single persons are present. I have heard of instances where a couple who expected a baby, told all their friends about it, but not a very close friend who happened to be unmarried or a couple that had no children. It also happens that marriage problems are discussed among friends, but that the conversation stops as soon as a single person walks in. They feel left out, not part of everyday life. This approach is often meant to avoid a painful situation, namely, not to discuss these matters in the presence of single people because they are not familiar with these kinds of things. However, to be left out in such matters of human life is felt as an even more painful experience. No one wants to be left out.

4. The task of unmarried members

The Form for the Solemnization of Marriage says that the Lord also today gives husband and wife to one another. We believe that the Lord gives everyone his or her own task and responsibility. No one should sit idle and wait until the Lord brings a partner to him or her. Each one has his own responsibility in this respect. And yet I believe that remaining unmarried can be something the Lord has in store for us. Some people really want to be married and, although they have waited a long time, they have not found the "help fit" for them. Such people may see the hand of the Lord in it, just as a couple which is married and does not receive children may know that also this comes from our heavenly Father. In the sight of the Lord their position, their task, and their mandate is not less important. The apostle Paul himself was unmarried, but he has been of great value for the kingdom of the Lord, and he has had many, what he called, spiritual children.

An unmarried person can be of great help in the work of the kingdom of God. Still, for some, especially for single women, it can be difficult. Their education has not always been geared to finding a full-time job for their whole life, because they had hoped to get married and to take care of a family. If they had known that they would stay single all their lives, they might have gone to university to get a professional education or taken some other form of specialized training. However, for men as well as for women counts what the apostle says in I Corinthians 7:17: "Let everyone lead the life which the Lord has assigned to him, and in which the Lord has called him." In the sight of the Lord there is no difference. The apostle Paul says in Galatians 3:28: "In Christ Jesus you are all sons of God, through faith." For in Him "there is neither male nor female; you are all one in Christ Jesus." And in I Corinthians 7:32-34 we read: "The unmarried man is anxious about the affairs of the Lord, how to please the Lord; but the married man is anxious about worldly affairs, how to please his wife, and his interests are divided. And the unmarried woman or girl is anxious about the affairs of the Lord, how to be holy in body and spirit; but the married woman is anxious about worldly affairs, how to please her husband." That does not mean, as it is interpreted by some Roman Catholics, that the unmarried state is of a higher level and greater purity and dedication than the married state, but it shows us certainly that there is a great task, also for those who did not marry. In the Lord they are certainly not less than others.

5. Having friends

A special problem for single persons is the point of living together with friends. It happens quite often that two girls or two older women are roommates and together run one household. Sometimes both have a full-time job and in the evening they do the housework together and cook the meals, or one of them has only a part-time job and takes care of the house. It even happens that they buy their own house together.

A comparable situation exists when two male friends live in the same apartment, or even when each has his own apartment but do spend most of their time together to study, to enjoy their hobbies, or just to have social contact and friendship. They may eat meals together as well. Although this is not wrong in itself, many consider this to be suspect. It seems to be okay to most people that two girls are roommates, but they are suspicious when two men share the same apartment. This is remarkable and can make life difficult for single men. They also need friendship, company, and social contact when they are lonely. However, no matter how they do it, it is suspect. If they share an apartment, people point a finger at them and label them homosexuals. If they take a female housekeeper, they are suspected of having an extramarital relationship.

Do we realize what kind of problems this causes for many of our fellow members? It has caused loneliness, grief and undeserved blame. It is certainly not so that homosexuality occurs only among men. We do not have statistics on it, but, going by my own pastoral experience and by the reactions and questions I have received from readers, I do not have the impression that homosexuality is less of a problem for women than it is for men. Although for female homosexuals sometimes the name *lesbian* is used, in this article I will use the word homosexual for both male and female persons.

Someone asked me to deal with the question: "Is it correct, is it wise, or is it probably wrong when two women share the same apartment and form one household, or even buy a house together, especially when the one has a full-time job and pays most of the expenses, while the other only has a part time job and takes care of the housework?"

If two women do not want to get married, perhaps even have an aversion to any form of sexual contact, are they then allowed to seek friendship and social contact together in their "own" household? It is an undeniable fact that they need friendship, support, and help in one way or another. They feel lonely and they can be of great help to each other.

The same counts for two boys or two men, although the public often reacts in a different way and is more critical when men are roommates than when women share an apartment. Before we can answer this question we have to say something about homosexuality and the implications of it.

6. Homosexuality

Homosexuality is an issue which is not very often openly discussed in our circles. It is so publicly and shamelessly promoted in the world and so fervently rejected and despised among our people, that little discussion takes place about it and, consequently, little is known with regard to the implications of it. However, that has caused a lot of misunderstanding about what really is going on. It has caused a lack of awareness of the problems which many of our members have to face. Most people do not understand what their problem is and how desperately they have to fight. Many have a completely wrong perception of what it is all about. Fortunately, some attention has been paid to this issue recently among our brothers and sisters in The Netherlands. People are becoming aware of the underlying problems. Brothers and sisters who need help and support in their struggle should not be left out in the cold but should be supported in fighting the good fight of faith. We have to condemn all homosexual practices, but at the same time we have to be aware of the struggle of brothers and sisters who fight against homosexual feelings all their life long.

In order to be able to understand the magnitude and the nature of the problem, we have to make a distinction between homosexual feelings and homosexual practices. Although the distinction is not so common in everyday language, we have to pay attention to the difference between what is called *homophilia* and *homosexuality* or between *homophiles* and *homosexuals*. Prof. Dr. J. Douma, professor of ethics at the Theological College of the Reformed Churches in Kampen, The Netherlands, gives the following definition: *Homophilia* is the condition in which people do not have the natural sexual desire but are largely or solely attracted to people of their own sex. *Homosexuality* is a sexual activity in which sexual acts with people of the same sex take place.

This definition shows that there is not only a distinction, but even a principal difference, between the two. The difference can be as great as the difference between fighting against sin and giving in to sin.

It has to be clear to everyone that the Bible condemns homosexual practices. Today people seem to be very lenient, and in some churches such practices are even openly condoned and propagated. Practising homosexuals, who publicly admit that they are living in this way, are allowed to serve as office-bearers in some churches. However, I am convinced that the Bible unequivocally rejects such practices. The apostle Paul, in Romans 1, calls it dishonourable passions and shameless acts, against which the wrath of God is revealed from heaven. About the people of Sodom and Gomorrah we read in Genesis 18 that the outcry of their sins was very grave. The LORD overthrew those cities after their wickedness had come to a climax in a demonstration of homosexuality and evil passions.

Over against all the modern theories which defend and condone homosexuality, we maintain and adhere to the clear testimony of the Word of God in Genesis 18 as well as in Romans 1.

However, having said this, we still have to consider the position of those who are homophiles, that is, those who have certain feelings but do not give in to these desires and who do not practise homosexuality. We should not underestimate the problems and the struggles of those who have to fight continually against a certain weakness or evil desire in their life.

Many brothers and sisters, members of our churches, are struggling with their problems, but do not dare to speak about them because they are afraid that they will be condemned and labelled, instead of being helped and supported in their fight.

I said already that there is a principal difference between homophilia and homosexuality. The former is a condition or inclination, a tendency, which does not necessarily mean any activity in this respect or any giving in to an evil desire. The latter means the practising of a sexual behaviour which is clearly in conflict with the Word of God.

Homophilia can be caused by a variety of things. It can be an innate disposition or it can be caused by circumstances or the environment. Often it is a combination of both.

Practising homosexuals can also be divided into two categories. There are those who give in to their innate feelings and intentions, their different disposition and inclination. This is known as core homosexuality. The second group is those who by the environment, the influence of their friends, or by other circumstances are involved in activities which they originally did not desire. They are homosexuals, not because of a natural inclination, but because of peer pressure, so that they finally become homosexuals, because their natural feelings are bent in a certain direction. This is often referred to as peripheral homosexuality.

There are classical examples of peripheral homosexuality. In the past it has happened that sailors lived together for an extended period of time with little room, little privacy, and almost no possibility of healthy entertainment. The same happened in times of war, when soldiers lived together in isolated positions, with very low moral standards. In such a men-only society the incidence of homosexuality increased and many "normal" boys were made homosexuals. The same can happen, for instance, in a factory where many girls are together in a sometimes boring environment. These horrible situations need no further explanation. We utterly reject and deplore such practices.

We face a more complicated and difficult situation when we deal with brothers and sisters who have a different predisposition and who must fight against it their whole life long. They are not homosexuals, but homophiles, and they need our help and support in their struggle. Let us not neglect them and make life even more difficult for them by ignoring their problem or — even worse — by ridiculing it. Let us keep in mind what the apostle says in Galatians 6:1: "Brethren, if a man is overtaken in any trespass, you who are spiritual should restore him in a spirit of gentleness. Look to yourself, lest you too be tempted."

Much more can be said about homophilia and the way it can be caused and stimulated or suppressed. However, may what has been said so far suffice for the time being to show that we have to make a clear distinction between homophiles and practising homosexuals.

7. Influence of the environment

Before we answer the question about two girls or women sharing one apartment, we first have to pay attention to another aspect of this matter.

It is impossible to divide people into two groups according to what has been mentioned before. It is not so clear-cut that we can say that one is a homophile and the other is not. A certain tendency or inclination may often be present, without ever becoming manifest. Many people are not even aware of such a potential hazard or inclination. Sometimes the circumstances can suppress such a feeling completely, so that it never shows up. In other circumstances it may be stimulated and developed. As we have seen before, it even happens that people who have hardly any innate tendency in this direction are made homosexuals because they have wrong friends or live in a bad environment.

Another aspect is that core homophilia can become manifest in two different ways — we can say: in a positive or a negative way. It can manifest itself in a positive way in attraction by and special affection for people of the *same* sex. It can become manifest in a negative way in an aversion to any form of relationship with members of the *opposite* sex. We can also call it the *absence* of *normal* feelings on the one hand, and the *presence* of *abnormal* feelings on the other hand.

In this respect, child abuse is a very important factor in the sexual development and predisposition of a person. As mentioned in another chapter, sexual abuse of children happens more frequently than we are aware of. In the majority of cases the perpetrator is not a stranger, but a father, an older brother, a good friend of the family, or a teacher. If such sexual abuse takes place between the ages of eight and twelve, or even younger, it always has consequences for the sexual development of the child. From pastoral experience, as well as from literature, I know that the victims often feel the consequences many years later, even in their own marriages. Many ministers and other counselors have been confronted with such cases. The result is often that the woman has a strong aversion to any form of sexual contact and considers it repulsive.

You may wonder why such people get married in the first place. The reason is that they are not aware of the fact that their feelings are "abnormal." They think it is something they have to get over. They either don't dare to discuss these matters with others, or, if they do, they are surprised to discover the magnitude of their problem and how great and lasting an impact the past still has in their present life and in the way they feel, react, and live together.

It also happens that a homophile is aware of his or her different feelings but still gets married to avoid being labelled and hoping that in marriage he or she will get over it. It happens that a genuine effort is made to handle the problem in this way. Provided that the matters have been discussed openly before marriage, it is sometimes possible for the partners to live in a Christian way and to be a help to each other in living according to the commandments of the LORD. If the matter has not been discussed before marriage, either because of naive ignorance or deliberately, it usually results in problems in the marriage, and these problems can only be solved with proper counseling by someone who accepts the commandments of the LORD and at the same time is knowledgeable and has experience in handling these delicate matters. Of course, whatever the situation, the couple must be prepared to work together to solve their problems.

8. Roommates

We are coming back to the question of the two single persons living together as roommates. Is it right, is it wise, or is it perhaps wrong for two girls or women to share the same apartment for an extended period of time?

We have to be careful not to generalize. We should not, mercilessly, treat all cases the same and condemn the one group of people for the sins committed by others. It is clear that those who never marry experience great loneliness. This feeling of loneliness often becomes stronger as they get older. They desire social contact, friendship, and communication, and we should help such people wherever we can.

Some people are very well aware of their homophilia. For such people it would be very dangerous to live together with a roommate. Homophiles are allowed to ask the Lord for help in their struggle. They may fall and rise time and again in their fight against sin. They have to fight against evil desires no less than everyone else against his or her weaknesses and infirmities. Their struggle is no less and not principally different from that of other members of the congregation. They also have to live by mere grace. They can survive and persevere only through the help of the Holy Spirit in their life. However, if such people go to live together with a roommate who may have the same feelings, they are exposing themselves to an irresistable temptation. It is a dangerous move which almost inevitably leads to homosexual practices. It is as foolish as when a boy and a girl, who are not married and who have normal sexual feelings live together as roommates, telling everyone that their relationship is strictly platonic. Even if they would try to live that way, it would create unacceptable temptations.

However, that two women, who had always hoped to get married, but remained unmarried, agree to share an apartment, is a completely different situation. There may not be the slightest trace of homophilia. They are only good friends and wish to have social contact and company. In such a situation I cannot see any reason why they should not be allowed to live in the same house and manage one household.

However, there is one thing we have to be careful about. I said already that homophile inclinations can be caused, stimulated, or activated by environmental conditions. Circumstances can cause something to surface that under different conditions never would have showed up. I mentioned the situations among sailors in the past and among soldiers in times of war, as examples. Anyone who has ever heard the language and tasted the atmosphere in a workplace where many girls are together, especially if they are working in a factory at a very boring job, knows how perverse the climate can be.

The circumstances are very important. Too close or intimate contact with someone of the same sex for an extended period of time can change someone's feelings. Something that always had been considered "unnatural" can become an acceptable substitute for what is out of reach. This danger is real and has to be taken into consideration.

Therefore, the answer to the question whether two women can live together cannot simply be yes or no. The answer is no if there is any awareness of homophilia. The answer is yes when there is not the slightest inkling in this direction. However, in all circumstances the parties have to be on the alert. As soon as they feel that something in their relationship is developing in a dangerous direction, they should not hesitate to part company. That can be done without destroying the friendship. A real friendship should be able to absorb the shock and to recognize and protect against any danger. It has happened that friends have parted from each other some distance, in order to continue their friendship in a proper way.

What has been said so far with respect to women and girls counts, in principle, also for men and boys. However, we have to face the fact that public opinion regarding male roommates is different from that with respect to females. There are also practical reasons why two men sharing an apartment is less likely. They usually have a different attitude with respect to housekeeping, and, if they really want to be married, it is easier for men to find a partner than for women. In our society the initiative is still supposed to be taken largely by the male partner.

We should not underestimate the problems and the loneliness of many single persons, also in our churches.

It is impossible to give clear-cut answers to all these questions. I hope that what I have said may be of some help, resulting in a better understanding of the existing problems, and serving as an incentive to help one another in these matters as brothers and sisters in Jesus Christ our Lord.

One final remark. In a discussion about the difference between homophiles and homosexuals someone made the remark that, if a homophile looks at a person of the same sex "lustfully," he has already committed this sin in his heart. Therefore every homophile is per definition a homosexual. This reasoning seems to make sense, at least it sounds logical. However, it can discourage brothers or sisters and put them down in their ongoing struggle to live according to he Word of God and to fight against sin. Of course, everyone who looks lustfully at his neighbour has already committed sin. In Matthew 5:28 Jesus declares: "But I say to you that everyone who looks at a woman lustfully has already committed adultery with her in his heart." However, it still makes quite a difference whether someone looks at his neighbour's wife or that he has intercourse with her. He who hates his brother sins against the sixth commandment, but it makes a great difference whether you speak evil of your brother or shoot him to death.

Let us listen to the Word of God as the only and ultimate rule for human life. We have to call sin *sin,* and we should not condone or defend any form of homosexuality. But at the same time we have to help and support those who happen to have very special problems in their life and who have to fight against certain weaknesses. A homophile who constantly fights against his evil desires may know in his struggle that the Lord is willing and able to give him the strength to persevere in the struggle, and he may give thanks to the Lord who helps him time and again to stay away from a practice which is against the Word of God. His struggle might be with falling and rising, praying for strength to finally overcome and reach perfection. (See Heidelberg Catechism, Lord's Day 52, answer 127.)

And all who feel lonely, forsaken, misunderstood, or misjudged by men, are allowed to know that we have a High Priest in heaven who is able and willing to help us. He will never forsake those who in true faith take refuge in Him.

CHAPTER FIVE

Some Aspects of Counseling

1. What is counseling?

In the four previous chapters we dealt with marriage, family life and divorce. Marriage and the raising of children are not always free of problems. Conflicts and friction do occur between parents and children and between husband and wife. Help may be needed to overcome the problems. The question is: Where does this help have to come from? Who is supposed to provide counseling? Do we, as Christians, have to go to a professional counselor or is it sufficient to ask the help of the office-bearers of the church? In this chapter we will pay special attention to some aspects of counseling.

Counseling is a current issue. We can hear about it everywhere. What do we mean by "counseling"? To *counsel* means: to advise, exhort, warn, admonish, or instruct. *Counseling* means: the act or process of giving professionally competent advice. That is what the dictionary says about it. Although every act of giving advice, admonition, and instruction can be called "counseling," we often use this word to indicate a professional way of giving advice to people who are confronted with situations they cannot cope with.

Such professional help can be given by a psychiatrist, a psychologist, a family physician, a social worker, or a pastor. The adjective "professional" in this respect means: given by a person who, by virtue of his profession, is supposed to give such help.

We have to make a clear distinction between counseling and medical treatment. Although they often go hand-in-hand, there is still a basic difference. We speak about medical treatment in all instances where medicines are given or prescribed. Such treatment may be given only by a physician. Counseling, however, is a method of helping in which no medicines are involved. The therapy includes only verbal means: listening, speaking, analyzing problems, and giving advice to solve problems, to change undesired situations, to admonish, to train, and to reprove.

Sometimes such counseling is given by a physician, either a family doctor or a psychiatrist. But often the counselor is a social worker or a pastor.

The fact that we include *pastor* in the list, along with *social worker* and *psychiatrist*, can make this issue a controversial one. Some argue that a Christian should never go to a psychiatrist. When someone is sick and needs medicines, he should see his doctor, but when he has mental, psychical, or spiritual problems, which can be solved by counseling, by discussion and advice, he should not go to such "professionals" who often are unbelievers, but he should go to the office-bearers instead. According to them, the best and the only appropriate medicine is the Word of God and prayer. The psychiatrist is often seen as an opponent or competitor of the office-bearers.

How hot an issue this is became clear, when an article by a Reformed psychiatrist was published in the Dutch daily newspaper, *Nederlands Dagblad*. He wrote about the position of psychiatric patients, their social problems, the support they need, and the way they are accepted by others. He discussed the general attitude that prevails in regard to psychical need and distress.

Six articles were submitted in response and as a reaction to his remarks. In those articles a divergency became manifest with respect to the approach to these problems. Many questions were raised. Is there really such a thing as psychical need and distress among Christians? Do we need and are we allowed to use the help of a specialist, or does a believer only need the gospel, the preaching of the Word of God, and the admonition of office-bearers? Isn't simple repentance and prayer the only legitimate and sufficient remedy for all such problems, at least as far as true believers are concerned?

The result was a number of "letters to the editor" (a total of 23!). The discussion was sometimes very confusing, and not all the arguments were to the point, to say the least. One point really struck me, and now I will quote from one of the letters: "If all these people, broken-hearted, with folded hands and bended knees, brought their needs before the Lord and expected their help from Him who knows all our problems and who is able to help, they wouldn't have to see a psychiatrist."

I must admit that this was not the general attitude. There were also quite a few who expressed their concern about such an approach. I mention this only to show how far some people apparently go.

Are we sufficiently aware of what is going on, and are we prepared to support and to cooperate in the proper way to help our brothers and sisters who are desperately in need of help? The statement: "I have never seen a true believer who had real psychical problems and who needed the help of a psychiatrist," is often a self-fulfilling prophecy as far as the experience of the speaker is concerned. That means: as long as someone propagates this approach and makes this point of view publicly known, people will never come to him with their problems, and he will never learn what is going on or experience what psychical need and distress is all about.

In this chapter I will deal with some aspects of counseling and try to find an answer to the questions mentioned above.

2. Soul and body

The words *psychiatry* and *psychology* are derived from the Greek word *psyche,* which means *soul* or *mind.* That is why some people consider it inappropriate to go to such a specialist. When we need help, comfort, or counseling for our soul, we should not go to a "specialist," but we should listen to the Word of God and ask the office-bearers for help. They are supposed to take care of our soul.

However, then, as in many similar cases, people go by what a word seems to mean rather than by what it really means.

The Bible uses the word *soul* quite often. It refers to our attitude towards the Lord and our spiritual life, as opposed to the word *body,* which refers to our physical existence. It is difficult to give you an exact definition. The meaning is not always the same. Generally speaking, we can put it this way: our soul is that which leaves the body when someone dies. That is how the Bible uses the word *soul.*

In psychiatry, however, the word *soul* or *psyche* is used in a different way and has a different meaning. Even though the same word is used it refers to a different matter. In medical terms the *psyche* is the human faculty for thought, judgment and emotion; the system of conscious and unconscious or subconscious reactions, feelings, and emotions.That system may function properly, or it may be in disorder, just as our intestinal system or our cardiac system can be in disorder.

We have to be careful that we do not identify the Biblical concept of *soul* with the medical concept of *psyche* or mind. We should not identify mental illness or disorder with a bad spiritual life. That would have strange consequences. Someone who is mentally very healthy can be spiritually dead, according to Biblical terms. And someone who is mentally ill can be very healthy spiritually. Sometimes mental illness and spiritual suffering go together, in the same way as physical and mental conditions interact, but that is not necessarily so, and we should certainly not identify the one with the other. That could have disastrous consequences, especially with respect to pastoral care and the support given to our brothers and sisters.

When we talk about psychical problems and disorders, we have to distinguish different categories of phenomena. In the first place there can be an organic defect, either as an innate deviation or caused by a trauma or accident. In such cases, particularly in the former, we speak of retarded, psychically handicapped or disabled persons. In professional circles further distinctions are used, but I will leave that out of the picture in this chapter.

It is very important to consider how we are supposed to approach such people and their relatives. Do we see them only as poor wretches, as a burden we have to live with? Do we encourage the parents and the relatives only by saying that they have to accept reality without complaints? Do we only say: it comes out of the Lord's hand, so you are not allowed to complain, and it does not help either? Or do we see the "handicapped" as our brothers and sisters in the Lord, children of the covenant, who received the same promises? Certainly, they are different, but not of less value in the sight of the Lord. Not useless, but perhaps of great importance and blessing for their surroundings.

What a lot of happiness, joy, and unity such children bring in their relatives' lives. That is what we have to notice and what we have to make people aware of with respect to psychically disturbed brothers and sisters. Keep in mind that disdaining and underestimating the value of such life is the first step on the way to therapeutic abortions and euthanasia.

It is very important to pay attention to these matters, and it would be worthwhile to dedicate a special chapter to the way we deal with the handicapped. However, for the time being I should like to focus on another aspect of psychical need and distress: not the organic defects in the first place, but the problems more or less caused by environmental influences, character weaknesses, loneliness, stress, and the like.

I admit that it is impossible to draw a straight line between organic and psychological aberrations and between physical and psychical diseases and deficiencies. Very often they are interwoven in a rather complicated way. On the one hand, for instance, a duodenal ulcer can be caused by lasting stress; according to some doctors, gallstones can be caused by unsolved frustrations, going back as far as infancy; the occurrence of a heart attack can be expedited by worrying too much. On the other hand, some psychical diseases or cases of mental disorder are caused by a chemical imbalance and insufficient secretion of some organs; that can have a poisonous effect on the cerebral functions.

With these restrictions in mind, I should like to discuss some questions concerning psychical need, distress, and disorder.

The first question we have to answer is this: Is there really such a thing as psychical need? At least, can someone who is a true believer have such severe problems that he needs the help of a psychiatrist, a psychologist, a social worker, or some other professional counselor, apart from the office-bearers? Is a minister allowed to call on such professional counselors for help, or is it enough and must it be sufficient to proclaim the gospel, to admonish, to comfort, to call to repentance, and to pray?

It all depends on whether we see the person involved as a patient, who needs help, or whether we consider his problem only to be a matter of sin and weakness in faith. I am convinced that the answer can be found only when we are fully aware of the fact that body and soul are a unity. We cannot and should not make too much of a distinction between organic and mental illness, between sickness of the body and improper functioning of the mind. They belong together; they interact and interfere constantly.

In a speech for the association of ex-psychiatric patients in The Netherlands, Prof.Dr.C.Trimp made this statement: "Why are people not ashamed of using aids like dentures or a walking cane while they are ashamed to go and see a psychiatrist?"

I hope it is clear that we cannot reject or condemn any professional help in cases of psychical need. But therefore the urgent question arises: What kind of help are we supposed to ask for?

With respect to counseling, different systems are propagated, and it is important to know something about the methods which are used.

3. Non-directive counseling

There is good reason to be suspicious about counselors. Truly neutral counselors do not exist. Every counselor has his ideas and a system in which he "believes." One system which is well-known and very often adhered to is the so called non-directive technique, also called the Rogerian system, after Carl Rogers, a famous American psychiatrist. His system is based upon the conviction that: "the innermost core of man's nature, the deepest level of his personality, the base of his 'animal nature' is positive in character — is basically socialized, forward-moving, rational and realistic."

According to him, every client is able to solve his own problems and he is the only one who has to solve the problems. The counselor should not give any directive, advice, or suggestion as to how the problems ought to be solved. The counselor is only supposed to listen, to show interest, and to "reflect" the feelings of the client in such a way that he becomes aware of what his problems really are. The counselor has to function simply as a sounding board or mirror, allowing his client to see himself and his problems. Sometimes he rewords what the client says in such a way that the client begins to understand his own feelings. To know that someone is really listening to him makes the client feel better already. A skilled counselor (according to Rogers) should be able to reflect the feelings of the client in such a way that he understands himself and that he feels he himself has found the solution to his problems. Rogers states that solutions given by someone else do not really help because they are imposed on the client. He will be really motivated to work on his problems and he will believe in the solution only if he has found it himself. That makes him feel independent and prepared to cope with every new problem as soon as it arises. The task of the counselor is to show the client his underlying feelings and to let him work out his problems by himself.

It is clear that in this whole concept little place is given to the consequences of sin in human life. The whole system is based on the humanistic point of view that a human being is good in himself. He only needs some help to find his own way in life, his own norms and standards, and to determine what is right and what is wrong. Basically, there is no general norm or moral standard: man is his own standard. Therefore little place is given to admonition, correction, or directive statements. What is good for the client is what is good. Anything that makes him feel happy is good.

Rogers mentions the following four points of difference between non-directive and directive counseling. A non-directive counselor

1. does not ask specific questions, but rather recognizes feelings and attitudes.

2. does not explain, discuss, or give information, but interprets feelings and attitudes.

3. does not persuade the client to undertake proposed actions, but leaves it up to him to act.

4. does not point out a problem or condition needing correction, but

reflects the client's feeling in such a way that he discovers his own problems and sees his responsibility.

It is clear that we cannot accept this system as the most appropriate way to help someone who is in trouble. It is even a dangerous approach, because it ignores the reality of sin. It gives in to the sinful desires of the client, as long as it makes him feel happy. What makes you feel good is good for you.

Over against this humanistic system of non-directive counseling, these so-called Rogerian techniques, some advocate the system of directive counseling — a system that involves telling the client what is right and what is wrong, and what he is supposed to do and what he should not do. This system is advocated, among others, by Dr. Jay E. Adams. In the rest of this chapter I will pay ample attention to his point of view.

4. Nouthetic counseling

Dr. Jay E. Adams calls his system "nouthetic counseling" or "nouthetic confrontation." The word "nouthetic" comes from a Greek word, used in the New Testament, among others, in Colossians 1:28, 3:16, and in Romans 15:14. It can be translated as: to admonish, to teach, or to instruct. However, according to Adams, it has such a special shade of meaning that he prefers not to translate the word but to introduce this Greek expression into his vocabulary.

With this word he refers to an approach by which the client is confronted with the Word of God. Sin is called sin, and the counselor is supposed to make clear to his client what he is supposed to do to get the problems in his life straightened out.

There are three specific aspects inherent in this word. The first aspect which Adams mentions is that it implies a problem and presupposes an obstacle that must be overcome; something is wrong in the life of the one who has to be confronted. In the second place, it refers to solving problems by verbal means, by speaking with the person, by teaching, by training and admonition. Thirdly, the purpose always has to be to help the client; everything is focussed on his benefit; this beneficent motive should never be lost and has to be prominent, according to Adams. [1]

In his book, *Competent to Counsel,* Adams makes strong points against non-directive counseling. The Rogerian system takes away the awareness of sin; if someone feels guilty, the counselor eliminates his bad feelings and gives him self-confidence instead. Nouthetic counseling (Adams says) does not take away the bad feelings but is intended to change the client's life in such a way that he overcomes sin. The patient does not suffer from guilt feelings (false guilt) but from real guilt. The counselor should not take away his feelings of guilt but change his sinful behaviour. [2]

Adams compares the Rogerian system with someone who takes a hammer to smash the red light on his dashboard which indicates that something is wrong under the hood of his car. To extinguish the red light does not solve the problem. It only takes away the possibility of acting in time and of preventing things from becoming worse. [3] He should not take away the warning signal but eliminate the danger about which the signal warned. In this respect Adams refers to James 5:14,15: "Is any among you sick? Let him call for the elders of the church, and let them pray over him, anointing him with oil in the Name of the Lord; and the prayer of faith will save the sick man, and the Lord will raise him up; and if he has committed sins, he will be forgiven." What James means to say, according to Adams, is that sin often causes sickness. Many sicknesses, and especially so-called mental illnesses, are caused by sins which are not confessed, either before the Lord or before man. Confession of these sickness-causing sins and prayer for forgiveness will save the sick man, and he will be raised. His mental as well as physical health will be restored. The oil, mentioned in this text, is considered the most common medicine used in those days.

Adams writes: "What James advocated was the use of consecrated, dedicated medicine. In this passage he urged the treating of sickness by medical means accompanied by prayer. The two are to be used together; neither to the exclusion of the other. So instead of teaching faith healing apart from the use of medicine, the passage teaches just the opposite. But when medicine is used, it must be used in conjunction with prayer. That is why James said that the prayer of faith makes the sick well. But James did not consider the use of medicine and prayer alone to be effective if the patient had committed sins. In such cases, prayer specifically must include the confession of sins. Sin is at the root of some illnesses and may at least be a contributing factor to some complications of other illnesses. And James further explained that confession must not only be made to God, but that sins must be confessed 'to one another.' Of course, confession is not an end in itself. Repentance and confession are but a means to reconciliation, which is the ultimate goal." [4]

Although Adams agrees that not all sickness can be seen as the result of sin or sinful patterns of life, he still puts great emphasis on sickness-causing sins and sin-engendered sickness, as he calls it.

He says many positive things in his book. He gives clear guidelines for directive, Biblical counseling. Many problems can be solved only if we are prepared to acknowledge sin as sin and if we are willing to amend our life, to listen to the Word of God, and to act accordingly.

In Christian counseling the client has to be encouraged to work on his problems and to solve them. One of Adams' basic statements is: "You can't say 'can't.' A Christian should say: 'I can do all that Christ asks me to do.' " [5]

Having expressed our appreciation for many things mentioned in Adams' book, I must also express my disagreement with certain points in his approach. As often happens when someone opposes a wrong system and fights against a dangerous theory, Adams goes too far in another direction, as we will see in what follows.

5. Sickness or sin?

On page 28 of his book, Adams calls mental illness "A Misnomer." That means: a wrong or unsuitable name given to something. According to him, mental illness does not exist. He puts it this way: "The Scripture plainly speaks of both organically based problems as well as those that stem from sinful attitude and behaviour; but where, in all of God's Word, is there so much as a trace of any third source of problems which might approximate the modern concept of 'mental illness'?"

Adams sees only two categories: organic malfunctions and sinful behaviour. Some so-called mental illnesses can be caused by organic malfunctions, but then there has to be a clear reason. He writes: "Organic malfunctions affecting the brain that are caused by brain damage, tumors, gene inheritance, glandular or chemical disorders, validly may be termed mental illnesses. But at the same time a vast number of other human problems have been classified as mental illness for which there is no evidence that they have been engendered by disease or illness at all. As a description of many of these problems, the term mental illness is nothing more than a figure of speech, and in most cases a poor one at that." [6]

Adams agrees that there is a correlation between psychological stress and illness, but then he sees the psychological stress as a result of sinful behaviour and as a sickness-causing attitude. He does not recognize sickness as a cause of stress and psychological problems. He argues that in many cases illness is pretended in order to cover up a sin or to escape the necessity of amendment of life. [7]

It is very important to realize the consequences of this theory.

Adams agrees that some so-called mental illnesses are caused by "organic malfunctions." He mentions, among other things, brain damage, a tumor, or a chemical disorder. But at the same time he states firmly that in cases for which there is no evidence that the disorder has been engendered by disease or organic malfunctions, we should not use the term "mental illness," but call it a result of a sinful attitude. He even states that, according to the Bible, there is not a trace of any source of "mental illness" apart from organic disorder or sinful behaviour. [8]

What does that mean? It inevitably brings us to the conclusion that in all cases where "no evidence" of "disease-engendered" phenomena can be given, the mental illness is a "sin-engendered" sickness. In other words: if no proof of organic malfunction can be given, the behaviour must be caused by sin.

This has far-reaching consequences for the way we deal with our sick brothers and sisters. Prof. Dr. C. Trimp mentions an important aspect and consequence of this reasoning. He writes: "That means that in the course of time, through the result of medical research, the territory of sin has been reduced considerably. A very incredible idea!" [9] What he means is this: The result of medical research has shown, in many cases, that there is an organic cause of mental disorder. Adams himself mentions chemical disorder. He even refers to cases of so-called "schizophrenic persons" who act strangely because they are seeing or hearing things which do not really exist. According to a recently published theory, this can be caused by a chemical malfunction, a so-called "adrenachrome" which disturbs eyesight or hearing. People hear and see things which do not exist. Adams calls this "perceptual distortion." His conclusion is: "a number of those who are currently labeled 'schizophrenics' could no longer be considered 'mentally ill' (as if their judgment were impaired), but would have to be reclassified as 'perceptually ill.' If perception is the problem, there is nothing wrong with the mental responses to what is perceived. If a book seems to be flying toward you (as your senses wrongly tell you it is), the right thing for the mind to do is to send signals to the arms to protect the head. Seemingly bizarre gestures, therefore, make sense when they are rightly interpreted as protective responses. If faulty depth perception wrongly tells you that something is about to bump into you, then for you to jog to the side suddenly is the correct thing to do. In other words, the counselee's mind is not sick; he is only seeing things wrongly and is, therefore, reacting in a proper way mentally to what he perceives wrongly." [10]

It might be an interesting discovery, but this story also tells us that a person who was previously "labeled" as someone who suffered from a sinful behaviour and a "sin-engendered sickness" all of a sudden has to be "reclassified" as being "perceptually ill." The sin, which previously was supposed to have caused his strange behaviour is replaced by an organic defect, and all this, thanks to medical research. Is that the way we are supposed to deal with our sick brothers and sisters? Does our admonition and accusation of sinful behaviour depend on the results of medical research? Do we blame the patient for his sickness until the doctor has found a reasonable explanation or an organic defect? Sometimes a physician may never find out what is wrong, and yet there can be a good reason why a patient acts the way he does. Is he therefore to be condemned as a sinner who suffers as a result of his own wrong attitude or unconfessed sins? That is what brought Prof. Trimp to the conclusion that, as a result of Adam's theory, the territory of sin seems to be reduced considerably by the result of medical research. Certainly an incredible idea!

I consider this to be one of the weaknesses of Adams' theory. It is even a dangerous point. Basically it means that, as long as we cannot see an organic reason for some abnormal behaviour, we are simply to blame the patient for his behaviour, and we are to call it "sin-engendered sickness," strange behaviour caused by a sinful attitude or a pretended illness used to cover up unconfessed sins. That is a very hard and merciless approach to brothers and sisters who suffer mental illness and who are desperately in need of Christian help and support. It is all a consequence of identifying the Biblical concept of *soul* with the medical concept of *psyche* or *mind*. This theory ignores the fact that a mind can be sick or in disorder just as well as any other part of the human body.

Adams agrees that there is "a grey area between, where it is uncertain to both whether a problem stems basically from organic or non-organic sources." [11] In his theory, however, he does not pay enough attention to this reality, and therefore he falls into the trap of generalization.

6. Mental illness

Mental illness does not exist, according to Adams. He knows only two sources: organic malfunctions and sin. It is "either-or." There is no in between. He states that the Bible does not give so much as a trace of any third source of problems.

I do not agree with him in this respect. His whole concept of "either-or" is incorrect. The Bible does not speak of such categories. The Bible does not give such a scheme, dividing all cases into two groups. Prof. Dr. J. van Bruggen, in an article in *De Reformatie* points out that in Matthew 4:24 among those mentioned who were healed by Christ were people with "various diseases." [12] A list is given there, and in that list "demoniacs" are also mentioned. Was that, according to Adams, an "organic illness" or was Matthew wrong in calling this a disease? And in Matthew 17:15 the sick boy is called an "epileptic" (or in other translations) "a lunatic." Was that an "organic" disorder or a "sin-engendered" illness? He was healed when Jesus cast out a demon.

In Matthew 8:16,17, we read that Jesus cast out the spirits with a word, and healed all who were sick. No distinction is made between "organic" and "sin-engendered" illnesses. Verse 17 says: "This was to fulfil what was spoken by the prophet Isaiah, 'He took our infirmities and bore our diseases.' "

Also in Luke 6:17,18, we read about "a great multitude of people from all Judea and Jerusalem and the seacoast of Tyre and Sidon, who came to hear Him and to be healed of their diseases; and those who were troubled with unclean spirits were cured."

Prof. van Bruggen, in his article, pays special attention to exorcism and the casting out of demons. That is not the same matter as we are dealing with here. However, what he writes is important also for our topic. He comes to the conclusion that the New Testament does not make a qualitative distinction between healing of the sick and curing of mental illness. [13]

The Bible does not make the sharp distinction between "organic" illnesses and "sin-engendered" sicknesses that Adams suggests. It is not a matter of "either-or." Sin is certainly involved, also in many organic illnesses. The Bible shows clearly that every healing of the sick was a matter of Christ's taking upon Himself our infirmities and our iniquities. But at the same time we have to be aware of the fact that not all cases of mental illness are caused by a patient's specific sin or sinful attitude.

Adams says: "The Scripture plainly speaks of both organically based problems as well as those problems that stem from sinful attitudes and behaviour; but where in all of God's Word, is there so much as a trace of any third source of problems which might approximate the modern concept of 'mental illness'?" [14] My answer to this suggestive question is: the Bible does not make such a clear-cut distinction between either organically based problems or problems that stem from sinful attitudes and behaviour. A human being is a unity, created by the LORD with a body and a mind. Both can be sick. It is even so that the two often go together and that the one affects the other. Physical illness is often reflected in someone's mental condition, and mental illness can disturb the proper functioning of the body.

We have to call for repentance according to the Word of God, but that should not be confined to people who are mentally ill. We should not approach a depressed person only with the message: "Repent, Believe in the Lord and you will be cured." Prof. Trimp puts it this way: "You could no more repent of apathy than you can of the flu." Mental illness and sin cannot and should not be identified with each other. We cannot repent of mental illness. Sin and illness are two different things and they belong in different categories. [15]

We also have to keep in mind that frustrations can have a strong influence on someone's mental development and the way he reacts to our approach. Prof. Trimp mentions the example of a boy who is very upset and frustrated because his father is an alcoholic. He hates his father. Too often he has been beaten when his father came home stone-drunk. Damage has been done to his "soul," and because of that he may react in an unusual way, at least according to those who do not understand his feelings. If an office-bearer should try to comfort him with the beautiful words of Psalm 103:13 he would become even more upset. "As a father pities his children, so the LORD pities those who fear Him" is something he does not understand. That is not a matter of unbelief or a sinful attitude. He simply cannot think about a father as someone who cares. He needs help and understanding to overcome his mental injury. [16]

When someone is deeply depressed or apathetic, it is not enough to say: "Believe in the Lord; rejoice in the Lord always. Your depression is 'sin-engendered'; that means: caused by unconfessed sins." That would be the kind of "help" Job received from his friends, but in the end the LORD showed how wrong they were. When we say such things to deeply depressed people, we make them feel even more desperate and no one should be surprised if they finally attempt suicide.

We have to be aware that a sick mind needs help no less than a sick body. That does not mean that an office-bearer is supposed to "refer" some cases to a specialist. He does not "refer" at all. He must continue his task, but a doctor should be involved as well. A pastor is supposed to visit and to help someone who suffers from a stomach ulcer, but that does not take away the necessity to see a doctor. And the fact that the doctor visits the patient does not make pastoral care superfluous. They have to work together. Both have their own task and responsibility, closely related, but different nonetheless.

7. Help from unbelievers

There is another aspect that must have our attention, and that is the question whether we can accept help from a psychiatrist or another counselor who is an unbeliever. While it is important whether a family physician is a believer or not, it is even more important when it is a psychiatrist or a psychologist who becomes involved or when counseling is received from a social worker. These people manipulate our minds. If possible we should look for help from a Christian counselor. But it is not always possible to find one. Therefore we have to take measures to prevent unnecessary damage and harm. And, fortunately, there are quite a few possibilities to work together with and receive help from people who are not true believers in the way we should like them to be.

There is one thing we have to keep in mind with respect to all doctors, and that is something very often forgotten or underestimated. The task of a physician, a family doctor as well as a specialist, is: to serve his patient. A doctor is subservient to the interests and well-being of his patient and not the other way around. A specialist has to adapt himself to the wishes and the preconditions of his patient. In the past the impression was sometimes given that the patient had no influence whatsoever and that he was not even allowed to ask questions or to be informed about details of his own health or the kind of therapy or treatment he was going to receive. He was not even allowed to get information from his own medical record. Fortunately, today there is better communication and most doctors are willing to listen and to take the feelings and wishes of their patients into consideration.

In my opinion, a pastor can play an important role in making people aware of their own task and position. When a Christian has to see a psychiatrist he has to make clear right from the beginning that there are some preconditions, like this: "I am a believer and my faith is not subject to discussion; divorce is not an option to solve my problems, nor is abortion." If he doubts his doctor's intentions, the patient can ask the specialist whether he is willing to help him under these conditions. It is up to the counselor to say yes or no. But my experience is that most doctors, also unbelievers, are willing to cooperate and to respect someone's feelings. But, of course, they first have to know about the feelings of their patients. How can a doctor respect someone's Christian life-style if he does not know about it? The problem is that people who need the help of a psychiatrist often are not prepared or able to speak up about these matters. Therefore it is important that the office-bearers give support, advice, and guidance; they can make people aware of these things and help them overcome these problems.

Sometimes direct contact between pastor and specialist is even possible. That depends on the circumstances and to a large degree on the personalities of the two: the pastor as well as the psychiatrist. Quite a few physicians are willing to cooperate and do discuss matters with the pastor — of course, never without the knowledge and consent of the patient.

It is clear that you have to be reasonable in such cases and that you have to accept certain limitations. Most doctors do not appreciate too much unrequested advice or too many suggestions with respect to the therapy.

There is one thing we should never ignore in this respect and that is confidentiality. We should never talk behind a patient's back. Confidentiality is a *conditio-cine-qua-non* for all proper and effective help.

Sometimes an office-bearer may hear things he is not allowed to report at a consistory meeting. The reason why people often don't open up is fear that their problems will become known all over the place. Of course, a consistory meeting is a closed session and no one is supposed to divulge what has been said there, but it sometimes does happen. A secret shared with so many people is no longer a secret.

8. Some practical cases

In conclusion, we should like to mention some practical cases to illustrate what has been said.

Very often a counselor has to deal with family problems, with disturbed or disrupted relations within a family, either between parents and children or between husband and wife. The one is often a result of the other. It is not always easy to find out what the real reason or cause of the conflict is. The people involved are not aware of the deeper background either. It takes a lot of effort, time, patience, and understanding to find out what is really going on. Quite often sexual problems are behind the scene. It is not, in the first place, the task of a pastor to solve such problems, nor is it his specific skill to counsel in such cases. Still it is extremely important to approach such cases in the right way, because they can have far-reaching consequences: unfaithfulness, extramarital relations, or even divorce can be the result.

A lack of support, bad counseling, or no counseling at all will make things worse. It goes without saying that such problems have an enormous impact on spiritual life. Sometimes problems reach the stage where people lose their courage and their faith and become completely desperate. Proper counseling is necessary to prevent things from becoming worse. In such cases so-called "nouthetic" counseling is necessary. We have to call sin sin, and we should not neglect or ignore the reality of sin and the necessity of repentance. But at the same time we have to realize that it is not enough to call for repentance. People often know very well that they are wrong, but they are unable to change their life and get rid of certain things without help. That is also a reality we have to face.

It may be necessary, then, to ask for professional help and counseling, not only by the pastor, but also by other professional helpers. It stands to reason that the choice of a counselor and his personal attitude is very important.

Another frequently occurring problem is alcoholism. It is a rather complicated matter; you have to find out why someone tries to escape reality by drinking. If you give advice, "Quit drinking," without trying to solve the problems behind the scene, you are like someone who mops up the floor without turning off the tap (in Dutch they say: *dweilen met de kraan open*). Don't underestimate the problems involved. Professional help is often needed to kick the habit.

Another problem is paranoid schizophrenia. Why is it that so many cases are becoming manifest these days? Did people change or is it only a matter of imagination? Neither is correct. The real reason is that in the past many cases were not recognized until it was too late — with fatal consequences. It is sometimes difficult to recognize or to find out what is going on. Especially in such situations, contact and cooperation with the person's physician is necessary. It is not easy to distinguish between religious problem, imagination, and psychiatric phenomena the first time one is confronted with a person suffering from this disorder. But, as we have seen, even Adams comes to the conclusion that schizophrenia can be caused by "organic malfunctions." I don't believe that an evident organic malfunction is a necessary precondition for acknowledging that a person is sick. Recent medical developments have shown that there is an organic reason behind many cases of mental illness. Probably more reasons will be discovered. However, that is not decisive. Pastoral care and the necessity of repentance do not depend on the result of medical research. We all need repentance, every day of our lives. But we also have to be aware of the fact that some brothers and sisters are sick and need help — psychical help — because they are mentally ill.

9. Conclusion

Finally, I should like to quote one of the letters to the editor, mentioned earlier, and published in *Nederlands Dagblad*. It was written in the form of a poem, and translated into English it reads like this:

No dream . . . . A crowded church
Text: Luke 17:11-17

"When the Lord saw her, He had compassion on her."
People had their judgment ready:
This widow must have been a terrible sinner . . .
Her husband had died
Now she had to bring
her son
to the cemetery.
The Lord must have had His reasons for that!
But: "He had compassion on her."

No dream . . . real history.
Job. Sitting in his misery.
His friends accusing him.
Eliphaz says: "Tradition proves
that the wicked will be punished."
Job cries: "Miserable comforters you are!"

No dream . . . a psychiatric clinic.
Eyes full of anxiety,
crying for help.
"Psychical need does not exist in the church,"
one says.
No help.
"Psychical distress is sin,"
another says.
No help.
Eyes full of anxiety,
crying for help.
"No need; don't ask a specialist,"
the next one says.
No help.

Don't dream!
Face reality!
Recognize the need and the distress
and help
professionally!

1 Jay E.Adams, *Competent to Counsel* (Grand Rapids: Baker Book House, 1982) pp.44-49.
2 *Ibid*, p.xxvii.
3 *Ibid*, p.95.
4 *Ibid*, p.108.
5 *Ibid*, pp.132-133.
6 *Ibid*, p.28.
7 *Ibid*, p.33.
8 *Ibid*, p.29.
9 Prof.Dr.C.Trimp, *Dienst*, j.g.30, nr.6, nov./dec.82, p.14.
10 Adams, *op. cit.*, p.39.
11 *Ibid*, p.37.
12 Prof.Dr.J.van Bruggen, *De Reformatie* j.g.58, nr.20, p.306.
13 *Ibid*, nr.21, p.321.
14 Adams, *op. cit.*, p.29.
15 Trimp, *op. cit.*, p.16.
16 *Ibid*, p.15.

CHAPTER SIX

Drugs

1. What are drugs?

Nowadays we hear about drug problems all around us. According to statistics, provided by the Ministry of Health, the majority of high school students have used marijuana at some time, and many are using it regularly. There is an alarming increase in the use of drugs at an earlier age. A great number of youngsters under fourteen years of age are already involved.

It is a well-known fact that the use of drugs became a problem in the army, especially during the Korean War.

In tackling this issue, it is important first to have a closer look at the meaning of the word *drug*. It is so generally used that we had better define what we are talking about.

The word *drug* originally comes from a word which means "to dry." In the past, pharmacists, physicians, and even primitive magicians, medicine-men, and witch doctors made use of all kinds of herbs which were dried. These dried herbs were used to make a medicinal tea, or an extract was made from them to prepare ointments or other "medicines." Today the word *druggist* is still used for a pharmacist. Originally, it referred to the man who selected and dried the herbs. Later this word was used not only for natural products but also for synthetic medicines. A pharmacy is still called a drugstore, and the word *drug* is used for all kinds of medicines.

However, for the purposes of this chapter on drug problems, I am restricting the meaning of the word *drug* to mood-modifying substances for other than medical purposes. Even with this definition we have to be careful, for what are "medical purposes?" Lots of people use tranquilizers, stimulants, or sleeping pills upon a physician's prescription. Some physicians are too lenient, prescribing refills on the patient's request even when there is no medical necessity. In this way the patient can become dependent on the drug or may even suffer more from the side-effects of the drug than from the disease itself.

The use of over-the-counter drugs is on the increase as well, and they are not always necessary for medical reasons either. Also in this respect we can speak about a drug problem.

2. Mood-modifying drugs

In the previous section I made reference to "mood-modifying" substances used for other than medical purposes. Let me first try to explain what is meant by *mood-modifying drugs.*

Three different groups of drugs can be distinguished by their effects. They are:

    a. *psycholeptics* or mind-restraining or mind-narrowing drugs.
    b. *psychoanaleptics* or mind-stimulating drugs.
    c. *psychodisleptics* or perception-changing drugs.

I should like to make a few remarks about all three of them.

It is not always easy to categorize a drug, because most drugs have side-effects and reverse effects. Besides, the reaction depends on many factors. It stands to reason that the reaction depends on the dose which is administered. Less commonly understood is the fact that the reaction depends on what the person expects from the drug. Whether the person is used to the drug, what his mental and physical condition is like, and many other factors also have an impact on the way a person reacts to a drug.

Take, for instance, the simple and very commonly used drug valium. In a small dose it works as a tranquilizer for most people. It makes one feel drowsy, sleepy, and relaxed. However, in certain circumstances, or with a larger dose, it can cause anxiety and restlessness; it can even make it impossible to sleep at all. That is called a reverse effect.

Drugs are categorized according to their most common and significant effects.

2a. *Psycholeptics* are mind-restraining or mind-narrowing drugs. This category includes most sleeping-pills and the major tranquilizers. Strong painkillers also belong to this group, especially the drugs derived from the poppy plant *(papaver somniferum)*. The best known of them are codeine, morphine and heroin. Alcohol belongs to this type of drugs as well.

Not all these drugs have the same strong effect. Some of them are simple "over-the-counter" type drugs. Painkillers with codeine are readily available without a medical prescription. Morphine is often used as a last-resort painkiller in the hospital. Heroin is rarely used in medicine. It is mostly an illegally sold and administered drug. Opium is sometimes used in medicines, but it is also a well-known and very old illegal drug. Most sleeping pills and tranquilizers are sold on prescription only.

What is common to all these drugs is that they give a certain feeling of calm, tranquility, and well-being, at least if they are administered in the proper way. Side-effects and reverse effects occur, especially when used without medical supervision.

Alcohol also belongs to this type of drugs. Although some people seem to think that alcohol can have a stimulating effect, the opposite is actually the case. The type of bravery and activity caused by the use of alcohol is only a matter of restrained awareness of reality. The mind is "impaired" and not able to register and react on all emotional and physical impulses.

2b. *Psychoanaleptics* have a stimulating effect upon the mind. They are also called "pep pills." The oldest medicine of this type is cocaine. It is derived from coca leaves *(erythroxylon coca).* (This name has nothing to do with Coca-Cola, which contains the stimulating substance "caffeine.") Another well-known stimulating drug is amphetamine. Its effect is much the same as that of cocaine, but it is synthetic. Its most remarkable effect is that it takes away the awareness of being tired. The suggestion that it makes people perform better physically or intellectually has been proven wrong. It only takes away the natural reaction of feeling tired.

Amphetamines were used during the Second World War. Aircraft crews who had to make very long trips, were given this drug to stay alert.

The use of such drugs needs very strict medical supervision to prevent fatal accidents. It is like removing all the red warning lights from the dashboard of a car. The car's driver will not be bothered by a signal that he will soon run out of gas, that his engine is overheated, that the oil pressure is low, or that the alternator does not work properly. He may feel comfortable, not aware of any trouble, but he cannot drive one mile farther than if all the lights were on . On the contrary. Without any warning, his engine will blow up beyond repair. The same can happen with amphetamines. The user feels happy and fit, capable of doing everything, until he collapses and his heart stops. He is burned out. The natural feeling of getting tired protects the body against exhaustion and overexposure. Taking away this mechanism of natural protection can destroy the human body.

Another drug which sometimes is categorized as stimulating is nicotine. However, it has a far smaller stimulating effect than amphetamines do, and it is even debatable whether nicotine should be listed as a stimulant. Under certain conditions and doses it can also work as a tranquilizer.

2c. *Psychodisleptics.* Most illegally used drugs belong to the perception-changing group of drugs. They induce a dreamlike or delusive state of mind. Perception is *changed* or *distorted*; the user does not hear, see, feel, and smell in the normal way. These drugs are also called *psychedelics* because the desired effect is often *intensified* perception and visual hallucinations, although in many cases these drugs cause precisely the opposite effects, such as anxiety, panic, and nightmares. Most users have had a so-called "bad trip" at one time or another.

The most common drugs in this group are LSD and cannabis. Cannabis is the genetic name of a product derived from the Indian hennep plant. As a drug it is available in three different ways: as marijuana, hashish, or "hash oil."

Marijuana is produced by drying the leaves and flowery tops of the plant. It is usually smoked as a cigarette or in a pipe. Some of its more popular names are: joint, stick, pot, grass, weed, stuff.

A more concentrated form of the same drug is hashish. This product is derived from the resin which covers the leaves and flowers of the plant. This resin is scraped off and packed into bricks. Small pieces of this product are mixed with tobacco or with marijuana and smoked.

Hashish can be concentrated into a liquid; it is then called "hash oil."

The concentration of the active drug THC (tetrahydrocannabinal) is about 5% in marijuana, about 10% in hashish, and sometimes up to 80% in pure hash oil.

The use of cannabis products is very old. It seems that the Chinese already used it more than 4500 years ago. In some literature we can read about emperors who gave their slaves hashish to make them willing and prepared to fulfil every assignment, especially to kill those whom the emperor did not like. These killers were called "hashishins." The English word *assassin,* for someone who kills for political reasons, still reminds us of these "hashishins."

The desired effect of cannabis is a feeling of well-being, excitement, joy, and cheerfulness, but depending on the condition of the user and the applied dose, unpleasant side effects such as fear, anxiety, dizziness, and even nausea and depression can occur.

LSD is a much stronger perception-changing drug. It was originally derived from a mould, growing on rye grain, but is now often synthesized. It causes all sorts of hallucinations. Visual, tactual, and aural perception are all mixed together. That means that the ability to see, to feel, and to hear is disturbed. The user gets the idea that he can hear colours, can see voices, and can feel smells. It is as if the wires are crossed between what he hears, sees, feels, and smells. Sometimes it is an exciting experience, but quite often the person on a "trip" ends up in psychotic distress, panic, and nightmares. And the result is that they try it again with a larger dose, simply to escape reality.

3. Addiction

In talking with young people about the dangers in using drugs and getting hooked on or addicted to drugs, we frequently hear the reaction: "Cannabis is not addictive. Someone might get hooked on heroin or LSD but not on hashish or marijuana. Even if you use it regularly, you can always stop if you wish. You will never get addicted to it." This answer shows that the person does not understand what addiction means and he does not know the dangerous stages that are involved in this process. At least five different aspects of addiction must be distinguished. They are:
  a. Habitual use
  b. Tolerance
  c. Psychological dependence
  d. Physical dependence
  e. Withdrawal
I will explain what the most significant symptoms are of these different stages.

3a. *Habitual use* is the first step on this devastating route. The person likes to use a certain drug simply because it makes him feel happy. It gives him a feeling of well-being. Although he might be able to quit, he does not want to. Even though he knows that the drug is dangerous, that it threatens his health or causes bad side effects, he is not prepared to give it up. We notice this habitual use also with people who smoke or drink too much. To a certain extent they are hooked on the drug. Although they can stop without any withdrawal effects, they do not want to. It has become too strong a habit. This occurs with *all* types of drugs.

3b. *Tolerance* is an aggravating factor in the process of becoming addicted. After a drug has been used for a certain period of time, the body gets used to its presence. The drug no longer has the desired effect, and a larger dose of the drug has to be taken to achieve the same result. This effect occurs with most drugs, although not to the same extent with all of them. Tolerance is a very dangerous effect, because it gives the user the impression that he is not addicted to the drug and that he can handle it without side effects. He can even do without it for a little while if he really wants to. But in the meantime his body has adjusted to the drug's continual presence and the user is ready for the next step on this slippery slope of dependence.

3c. *Psychological dependence* means that a person is so used to a drug and its effects that he is in constant emotional need to continue taking the drug and experience its effects. Without proper help he is not able to stop. He has become dependent on the drug, and he is not able to make a reasonable and critical evaluation of his own situation. He may even lose control over his own determination with respect to the frequency and the dose he is going to take. This psychological or emotional dependence occurs sooner or later with *all* drugs. Alcohol, sleeping pill, nicotine, hashish, and marijuana users develop a strong dependence on these drugs, while dependence on heroin, cocaine, and amphetamines become stronger still.

3d. *Physical dependence* is the next step. When tolerance has developed and the dose has been increased for some time, the body reaches a stage in which it can only function properly while the drug is present. The drug does not have the desired effect any longer, but absence of the drug causes adverse effects. Physical dependence occurs especially with drugs like alcohol and sleeping pills and is very strong with drugs like heroin, morphine, and codeine.

3e. *Withdrawal* is the effect a person experiences when he has become physically dependent and then suddenly stops taking the drug. The body is used to the drug and produces an antidote. When the person stops using the drug, the body still produces the antidote, but because of the absence of the drug, the person suffers strong reverse effects. Instead of a feeling of well-being, joy, and cheerfulness, he experiences depression, anxiety, nightmares, and complete physical disorder with nausea, shivering, and other sometimes life-threatening symptoms. Without proper medical help and supervision, it is humanly speaking impossible to withdraw.

4. Some statistics

To give you an idea how widespread the use of these drugs is, I quote from a brochure made available by the Ministry of Health of the Province of British Columbia.

"According to one recent study, approximately one in twelve adults has experimented with cannabis use. A study of 124 public and private high schools in the United States, prepared for the National Institute on Drug Abuse over a period of three years and released in 1978, showed that 56% of students surveyed had used marijuana at some time, 48% in the past year, and 35% in the month prior to the survey.

"A survey carried out in Vancouver public high schools, the third in a four-yearly series, indicated that of the students surveyed 44.7% had used marijuana at some time, 37% in the six months preceding the survey, and 20.3% in the 30 days preceding the survey.

"The survey showed that cannabis use is starting at an earlier age. In 1970, 9.9% of those under 14 reported they were using cannabis, as compared with 14.2% in 1974 and 17.8% in 1978."

These are statistics about students in public schools. Let us not fool ourselves, thinking that these things do not happen among Christians. Too many parents do not believe that their children are involved, until they find out the truth and get the shock of their life.

Up to this point in this chapter, I have provided information. For some of you it may be a little too "technical" or too "medical." It is very important, however, to be familiar with the ins and outs of the matter, before we come to an evaluation of the problem. In what follows we will have a closer look at the moral and ethical aspects of it and take a stand in this matter.

5. A general problem

In discussing the problem of drug abuse and drug addiction, we have to realize that this is not just a problem of young people or of the "lower class." On the contrary. It is a general problem, closely related to our modern society and its affluence. It is a result of luxury, wealth, and a lack of moral values.

Especially when we realize that alcohol, tobacco, tranquilizers, and sleeping pills belong to these drugs as well, we will know how common the problem is. It would be hypocritical to eliminate alcohol and tobacco from this list. A great number of people, also highly respected persons, are addicted to cigarettes and are unable to quit smoking, although the health hazard is undeniable. In all kinds of families and at all kinds of parties too much alcohol is used. Not only the recognized alcoholic is addicted to drugs, but in many cases the so-called "social drink" becomes "habitual use," to such an extent, even, that people lose control of their faculties for a while. Things are done, said, and tolerated, which in "normal" circumstances would be considered improper and unacceptable. We are dealing here with excessive use, and in many cases it is a form of addiction to drugs. It is a losing battle to fight the abuse of and addiction to drugs among the young people, as long as we do not recognize this problem and reconsider our personal attitude about these matters.

In the past the use of alcohol was found especially among poor people, in the "lower class." They tried to forget their problems and to find comfort in their habitual drink. Nowadays excessive drinking has become a generally accepted phenomenon, even a "status symbol." Also excessive use of tranquilizers and sleeping pills has become part of modern life.

Affluence has not brought happiness. Instead it has made life meaningless and empty. The older generation indulges in luxury, apathy, and normlessness, but they are not happy. Many live a double life. They keep up appearances, but in the meantime, behind the scenes, it is like an apple rotten at the core. Broken marriages can be found everywhere, and corruption and indecency pops up also among prominent people, up into the highest ranks. Many young people are watching this development with amazement, and it turns them off. They consider such a society hypocritical, and they have their own solution. Life does not make any sense to them. They try to escape reality; they try to find comfort and happiness in a world which they know is not real, but at least is more attractive to them than reality.

6. Peer pressure

Although many young people (and also adults) pretend that they do not care about what others say or think about them, the opposite is true. Peer pressure and the desire to be part of the group is a very strong factor in the general pattern of behaviour. No one likes to be singled out. Young people, especially, are very eager to be popular, respected, and esteemed by their friends. The aspect of social acceptance is much stronger than we often realize. That also counts for the use of drugs. The environment is extremely important. Most children do not like a drug and its effects the first time they use it, because it makes them sick, but the peer pressure prevails. A marijuana cigarette (a stick) is passed on from one to the other (a joint stick). Those who refuse to join this group event are teased, and because they do not want to be spoilsports, they give in — not because they like the drug or desire its effect, but simply because they cannot withstand the peer pressure.

Parents should be aware of this effect. They have to show their concern in at least two ways. In the first place, they have to watch the environment in which their children are living: the school they attend as well as the friends they have, the places they go to for entertainment as well as their job sites. In the second place, parents have to speak very openly and frankly with their children about these things. They should try to help them to overcome the peer pressure, or, even better, to reverse the effect. In sticking together with the proper friends, and supported by their parents, young people can use peer pressure to go in the other direction, namely, to stop the spread of drug abuse and to discourage others from taking part in it. However, in order to be able to do so, parents have to be aware of what is going on. Closing their eyes to reality does not serve any purpose; it only makes things worse.

7. Slavery

Drugs are often presented as something that makes one feel free, relaxed, happy, and joyful. They supposedly let people forget the dullness of everyday life for a while and give them a "kick." Some even believe that a "trip" makes them better able to function in normal life. That might be true to a certain extent for sleeping pills, used under medical supervision. To have a good night's rest is helpful and necessary to function properly in daily life. However, taking sleeping pills should never be done without medical supervision, in order to avoid addiction and undesired side effects.

This can never be said with respect to illegal drugs. The drug may induce a dreamlike feeling, but it can never replace or change reality. It only causes the user to feel even more miserable afterwards. When someone uses drugs to escape reality and to forget the misery of his actual situation, he will only fall back into greater distress. Instead of feeling relaxed and being set free, he is enslaved by the drug. He has to take a new and ever larger dose. Reality becomes more and more frightening, and finally he reaches the point of no return.

The drug seems to give relief and entertainment, but it is actually a matter of losing control of one's own faculties. The user has become a slave instead of a human being. Someone compared the effect of using drugs like cannabis and LSD with driving a car with a broken steering shaft. With this car you can drive in any direction, but you have no control over it. It is very unlikely that the car will take you where you want to be. That is a dangerous and life-threatening situation.

8. Professional help

A person who is addicted to drugs needs help. That counts for every stage of addiction: for the habitual user as well as for those who are physically dependent. What the most appropriate type of help is depends on the circumstances.

Sometimes the question is asked: Does a drug user need the help of a professional counselor or the help of the office-bearers in the church? Is it a matter of sickness which has to be cured by the doctor, or is it a matter of sin which can only be "cured" by admonition, prayer, and repentance?

These questions are wrong. This dilemma should not be made. It is not a matter of "either-or." It is not "the one or the other." Of course, someone who is addicted to drugs is sick. There may be withdrawal symptoms which need medical treatment. The person also needs professional assistance to cope with all his problems. But at the same time we have to realize that sin and sickness in these cases are so closely related and interwoven that no doctor can really cure the problem. Real comfort and peace of mind for those who are desperate can only be given by Jesus Christ. The misery of human life can be taken away only by a true faith in Him. Let us not separate the physical and the spiritual help. To say to one who is addicted to drugs: "Pray and stop using drugs," is just not enough. To say to an alcoholic: "Quit drinking," does not really solve his problem. Real help requires the cooperation of all available helpers. Parents and office-bearers have to comfort, support, and admonish the addict. The environment has to be changed, as much as possible, in order to make it easier for the addict to stay away from the temptation. At the same time the help of a physician or a professional counselor may be advisable, depending on the stage of addiction and the side effects caused by the drug, or the withdrawal symptoms caused by the absence of the drug.

Let us try to work together in an effort to help, to save, to bring back to the flock those who are in danger of going astray.

9. Prevention

There is an old saying: "An ounce of prevention is better than a pound of cure." If ever, this is true with respect to drug abuse. When someone has started to climb the ladder, or rather, to go down the slippery slope of drug abuse and addiction, it is extremely difficult to stop the process or to reverse the course of events. That counts for someone who starts smoking normal cigarettes as well as for someone who tries his first "joint stick." Therefore we should try, in the first place, to prevent younger and older people from beginning to use drugs.

The most important defence against addiction, and the best way of protection, is the preaching of the gospel, the message of Jesus Christ, who really sets free from slavery and gives joy, strength, and a new future. The message of the gospel makes clear to us that life really makes sense and that it is worth living. When we see our riches in Jesus Christ, we know that the future is not dark and meaningless. No matter how difficult the present situation may be, we have a prospect, a future, to look forward to. Someone who really trusts in the Lord and takes refuge in Him does not need an "escape" from reality into the world of drugs. The Word of God gives us a comfort and a freedom, a joy and a "tranquility" which far outweighs the deceptive world of drugs.

In this respect, the example of parents is very important. Parents have to *show* that what they teach their children is not just nice talk, but a living reality in their own life. Youngsters are often very sensitive in these things. A life-style which contradicts this teaching makes the parents lose credibility with their children.

When parents warn and admonish their children with respect to drug abuse, but at the same time are heavy smokers who cannot get rid of their habit, although they know how dangerous and unhealthy it is, the children will not be impressed by their testimony. The same is true when parents make excessive use of alcohol at their parties at home. We are not supposed to live as ascetics, like monks in a monastery. We are allowed to enjoy life with all the good things the Lord has given us. But we also have to show self-control and restraint in everything we do. In I Corinthians 7:30 the apostle Paul says: "Let those who rejoice live as though they were not rejoicing, and those who buy as though they had no goods, and those who deal with this world as though they had no dealings with it. For the form of this world is passing away."

We are allowed to use all the gifts the Lord has bestowed upon us, but we should never let these things rule over us. That should be our attitude and our approach in all areas of human life.

10. Setting an example

In his book, *Christelijke Ethiek* (Christian Ethics) Capita Selecta II, Prof. Dr. J. Douma mentions the fact that the misery caused by the use of alcohol and tobacco is much greater than the number of casualties caused by dangerous drugs like morphine and heroin. The number of people who die because of an illness caused by smoking is many times greater than the number of people killed in traffic accidents. It is a generally recognized fact that the smoking of tobacco constitutes a health hazard. Therefore we should try to do away with this bad habit.

That cannot be achieved overnight. A radical attitude in this respect will not achieve the desired effect. We should try to convince youngsters not to start with this habit at all. In this way the next generation will, in this respect, hopefully be wiser than the present generation.

This goal can only be reached if the parents are willing and able to set a good example. It would be a step in the right direction if smoking could be abolished and banned from all schools, public buildings, trains, streetcars, buses, and the like.

In this respect the churches should take the lead by banning smoking from all church properties and ecclesiastical meetings.

I fully agree with Prof. Douma in this respect. We can complain and voice all kinds of concerns about the increase in drug abuse and addiction. But it does not help, it does not convince, and it sounds almost hypocritical, as long as we are not able to start the battle at home, in our own life.

11. Conclusions

a. The problem of drug abuse and addiction is not just a problem of some young people who smoke pot, nor is it restricted to people of the "lower class." It is a general problem.

b. Not only marijuana, hashish, LSD, and that type of drugs are dangerous and addictive. Also tobacco and alcohol belong to the drugs which are threatening our society and human life in general.

c. Addiction is not a simple phenomenon which occurs with some drugs and not with others. It is a process with different stages. Not with every drug are all the stepping stones obvious. And yet, with all drugs some form of addiction develops.

d. The underlying cause of the whole problem of drug abuse is the apathy of affluence, the normlessness, and the lack of purpose in life.

e. Real freedom, happiness, and joy in life, in spite of the difficulties which may exist, can be found only in Jesus Christ. Through Him life makes sense, serves a purpose, and has a destination.

f. Those who are overpowered by the spirit of darkness and are bound in slavery of mind through drug abuse, can be saved only through Jesus Christ and the work of the Holy Spirit.

g. We have to use all available means to help those who are addicted to drugs. In the first place, the message of the salvation through Jesus Christ. At the same time we should use the necessary medical and other professional help to set them free from this spiritual and physical trap.

h. We should not only treat the symptoms, but first and foremost fight the cause. We have to work preventively and try to keep our youngsters away from drugs and the environment which can cause them to use drugs.

i. Parents have to discuss these matters openly with their children. They have to be well aware of what is going on. Only in this way can they help them to stay away from these disastrous substances.

j. As Christians we have to set an example. Evangelism is important, but our walk of life should be a clear testimony in the first place.

k. To ban smoking out of our life as Christians and to reduce our (too often excessive) alcohol consumption should be the first step to fight the increasing abuse of and addiction to drugs.

l. We are allowed to use all the beautiful gifts which the Lord has given us, and we may enjoy life in this world, but we should never let these things rule over our life and overpower us. We know that real joy, happiness, and lasting comfort can be found in Jesus Christ alone.

CHAPTER SEVEN

The Borderline of Human Life

1. Between life and death

In this chapter we will discuss some matters concerning the borderline of human life. We will deal with questions which arise when people are on the verge of death.

That does not seem to be a cheerful topic. Some may wonder why we have to discuss such a matter extensively in a book like this. Isn't death a reality we have to live with and to accept? From a Christian point of view we can see it as an inevitable consequence of sin. It will be with us until the end of this world. But need it be extensively discussed?

I think it is important to pay attention to a number of points which may often be overlooked, or at least not dealt with properly. An open discussion of these things can make it easier to deal with problems which otherwise could cause frustration.

That there are important questions to be answered becomes clear when we realize that people are apparently not able to agree even today, on the question of what death really is. That may sound somewhat strange. Everyone knows what death is; we are all confronted with it in one way or another, aren't we?

Still there is increasing insecurity with respect to the borderline of human life. When exactly does it end? Even in the medical field people are looking for a solid and satisfying definition. I will try to explain what is really at stake.

In the past it was sufficient to ascertain that the patient had stopped breathing or that the heartbeat had come to a halt. Today neither of these phenomena are decisive any longer. When a patient stops breathing, it is possible to use a respirator to continue his breathing artificially. That the stopping of the heartbeat cannot be considered either as evidence of being dead will be understood when we realize that people can live with an artificial, purely mechanical heart. Sometimes a patient lives for many hours, while his heart has been stopped for open heart surgery: an external heart-lung machine takes over the heart and lung functions.

We will see later what consequences this has with respect to organ transplants. For the moment, may it suffice to prove that neither the absence of breathing nor the stopping of the heartbeat can serve as sufficient proof that someone has passed away. We need other evidence.

Of course, in most cases it is very clear that someone's life came to an end. However, especially with people who were involved in an accident, who are in a deep coma and on a monitor, a respirator, or other life-saving devices, it is sometimes questionable whether they are dead or not. What is the difference between a person in a deep coma, supported by life-saving devices in an Intensive Care Unit, and a dead body in which the flow of blood, the heartbeat, and the breathing are kept going artificially?

When we think about this for a while, our conclusion must be that we are confronted with the mystery of human life.

2. The wonder of human life

Psalm 139 speaks about the wonder of human life. "For Thou didst form my inward parts, Thou didst knit me together in my mother's womb. I praise Thee, for Thou art fearful and wonderful. Wonderful are Thy Works! Thou knowest me right well; my frame was not hidden from Thee, when I was being made in secrect, intricately wrought in the depths of the earth. Thy eyes beheld my unformed substance; in Thy book were written, every one of them, the days that were formed for me, when as yet there was none of them." Knit together by the LORD, intricately wrought. That means: complicated, containing many detailed parts, difficult to understand.

Human life is a wonder. Every human life is mysteriously created by God's hand. We hold to that even in a time when people talk about genetic engineering and test-tube babies. Life comes from the LORD; it is created and maintained by Him from the very moment of conception. People try to unravel this mystery. They try to gain control of it and to imitate it. Some see human life as a remarkable development of DNA chains, a biochemical process that can be brought under control and can even be manipulated by men. They are already talking about "raising" or "creating" a special breed of human beings, with special characteristics, according to the wishes of the man in the laboratory. I will deal with this issue separately in another chapter.

We shouldn't say too hastily that such a development is impossible. We don't know what will happen. The Bible teaches us clearly that the devil will come " . . . with all power and with pretended signs and wonders, and with all wicked deceptions for those who are to perish . . . ." (II Thessalonians 2:9, 10). And in Revealtion 13:15ff. we read about the devil who was allowed to give breath to the image of the beast so that the image of the beast should even speak. That means: a dead image is caused to speak and to act as a human being. It seems to be the creation of human life out of a dead image. Those are really deceptive signs and pretended, even pretentious, wonders.

We don't know what will happen and what almost-miraculous things human beings will be allowed to perform. It may be almost unbelievable and inconceivable. But don't worry too much. II Thessalonians 2:9 says that they are "pretended" signs and wonders — a lot of pretence without real substance. And, moreover, the devil will never be allowed to go one step further than the Father permits him to go. Jesus Christ Himself has said in John 10:28,29, concerning those whom the Father has given Him that no one can snatch them out of the Father's hand and out of His hand. Don't panic when you see unbelievable things. Trust in the Lord our God and in Jesus Christ who stays in control.

However, one thing we know for sure: life comes from the Lord; we have to hold to that. We do not speak about the absolute value of human life, we do not consider the human right to life a universal human right. Instead we speak about the right of the LORD, the Creator of human life. He is the only one who, sovereignly, can decide on or dispose of human life. He gives life and He can take it away. He makes it begin and He can let it come to an end. Every decision or action of men with respect to human life has to be subject to His commandments. That is what we have to remember when we talk about abortion. Human life is a work of God's creating power, right from the very moment of conception. Every destruction of or infringement upon this life is an act against the LORD. We do not speak about the absolute value of human life — neither with respect to the beginning, nor with respect to the termination of it. We *do* speak about the absolute right of the LORD with respect to human life. That also counts when we hear about eugenic abortion.

3. Eugenic abortion

Eugenic abortion is an abortion executed "to improve the human race." During pregnancy, a test can be performed to see whether the baby may be handicapped, retarded, or suffering from other abnormalities. If so, an abortion can be performed to prevent the birth of the baby. We all agree that in such a case a human being is killed. In principle, it doesn't make too much difference whether the baby is killed before or after birth. Therefore we should be careful with regard to such tests. It can bring a family into temptation to violate the rights, not of a human being, but of the LORD, who created life. This is especially so when they have to deal with a doctor who tries to make them believe that they are doing the right thing. Sometimes it seems to be difficult to go against the advice of a physician, even when he is an unbeliever and tries to make us act according the ethics of atheists rather than according to the commandments of the LORD.

However, we should not treat all cases the same. We have to make a distinction between eugenic abortion and abortion upon medical indication. The latter often refers to an abortion performed to save the life of the mother. Is that acceptable? According to the ethics of the Roman Catholic Church, the life of the baby always prevails over the life of the mother. Even if, humanly speaking, it can be expected that the mother will not survive the delivery, the life of the baby comes first.

To come to a proper choice in this dilemma, we have to be careful in our formulation. We shouldn't use the word abortion at all in this respect, although it might be the appropriate technical term in medical jargon.

The aim and purpose of every medical treatment has to be to save the life of the patient or to relieve his suffering. Risks have to be considered. That is the responsibility of human beings who face a difficult decision. After an accident, for instance, the lives of a number of people can be in danger. Risks have to be taken to rescue them. That can put people in a threatening dilemma. The rescue of one can increase the risk for, or even kill, another. A choice has to be made. Serious consequences are inevitable both ways. That is a precarious situation, but nonetheless we have to act. Doing nothing may cost two lives, while, humanly speaking, one life can be saved.

The same situation can occur during a pregnancy or a delivery where, going by the information which is available and the consequences as far as they can be foreseen, the life of the mother can be saved only at the cost of the life of the baby. We should not call this an abortion. The crucial point in this respect is that the intention of the treatment is to save the life of the mother and not to terminate the life of the baby. If the consequence of this life-saving operation is that the life of the baby has to be sacrificed, it is part of an inevitale choice, rescuing one out of two human lives.

It is clear that we cannot speak about the absolute value of human life. We have to be obedient to the Lord and we have to repect His sovereign and absolute right with respect to human life.

In such a situation we have to make a distinction between the "relative value" of two lives. It can happen that someone has to sacrifice his life to save the life of others. For instance, in time of wars, in calamities, or in rescue operations a commander-in-chief may have to make a decision to sacrifice the life of some, in order to save, rescue, protect, or defend others. In the same way it can be necessary to sacrifice the life of an unborn baby to save the life of a mother who is supposed to take care of a family and who still has an important task with regard to the rest of the family. We cannot escape such decisions, and we should not try to evade them either. In this respect we have to bear in mind that we are not dealing with the absolute value of human life, the right to life, or other human rights, but with the God who creates life. We have to make decisions which can stand the test of His Word. We have to face our responsibility before Him, the God of life and death.

However, to prevent misunderstanding, it has to be stressed that cases like this very rarely occur with the present state of medical help. Situations where a choice has to be made to save the life of the one at the cost of the other are few in number.

What I have said so far about abortion and making a decision with respect to a treatment that has a desired effect but also some undesired effects or undesired consequences, is important with regard to euthanasia as well.

4. Euthanasia

Euthanasia is an issue which is receiving more and more attention. We have to think about the implications, and we have to discuss the ethical aspects of it. Of course, we can say; "We are against it! Period!" That is an easy way out, and we are in danger of evading the real questions. We have to be aware of the problems and the complexity of this issue.

A distinction has to be made between passive and active euthanasia. That, in itself, shows that we cannot treat every case the same.

What do we mean by active and passive euthanasia? In short, we can put it this way: active euthanasia is doing something to terminate human life, while passive euthanasia is causing someone's death by deliberately leaving something undone. However, this matter is much more complicated than it might seem at first glance. Therefore I will explain some aspects in what follows.

The word *euthanasia* comes from a root which means: to die in a desirable way. Literally it means: "a good death." Its original meaning expressed the desire to die in a peaceful and painless way, without suffering and anxiety. According to ancient literature, Caesar Augustus prayed that he should die without suffering and pain. That was "euthanasia."

Nowadays the word is understood to mean: to cause the death of a patient who is incurably ill, handicapped, retarded, or in terrible suffering — at least to hasten his death. It is done on request of the patient himself or, if he is unable to make a decision himself, on request of his family.

We reject every treatment or action undertaken with the purpose of bringing human life to an end. It does not matter what kind of human life it is. It is not up to us to decide whether human life is still meaningful. Even with incurably ill, demented, or severely handicapped people, it is not up to us to decide about their span of life. We cannot judge about the meaning of their life. We should not ask questions like: Does it make sense? Does it serve any purpose whatsoever to keep them alive? It is not up to us to decide! Life comes from the LORD and He, our God, the Creator of human life, is the only one who has the right to terminate or to take away human life. Our judgment on the quality of human life, on its usefulness or uselessness, does not give us the right to intervene.

The fact that people are unable to communicate because they are in a deep coma or in a state of lasting unconsciousness through heavy sedation does not give us the right to make decisions about the end of their life. With respect to severely handicapped, demented, imbecilic, or idiotic people, we have no right to decide whether their life is meaningful either. We know that handicapped people can be a real blessing in a family and can create a better atmosphere of unity, communion, and willingness to serve, than can be found in many families with so-called superintelligent children.

Active euthanasia, in whatever circumstances it takes place, is always a violation of the commandments of the LORD; it is a matter of killing our neighbour. Passive euthanasia is a more complicated matter.

5. Passive euthanasia

The term *passive euthanasia* refers to a situation in which something deliberately is left undone that, humanly speaking, could have prolonged life. Here we enter a very precarious area. What do we mean by prolonging a life? We should have respect, not for human life as such, but for the God who creates human life. That means that we also respect God's deeds with regard to the termination of human life. On the one hand, we can see everywhere how people take into their own hands the decision to kill others. But, on the other hand, many are not prepared to face death as a reality, when it comes at a time decided upon by the Lord.

In hospitals we can see doctors fighting desperately against death, unwilling to admit that it is the Lord who decides. Especially with respect to some heads of state we have heard strange stories about doctors, who were unwilling to give up a — humanly speaking — lost battle. That borders on idolatry. We shouldn't take away someone's "right to live," but we should not infringe upon someone's "right to die" either. We would do better to state it this way: we have to accept and to respect the Lord's hand in creating and maintaining human life as well as in bringing it to an end. Refraining from further treatment in such cases is not passive euthanasia. It is a matter of facing reality, of admitting that life is not something we can decide on.

In this respect I am not only thinking about circumstances in which further treatment finally results in a desperate continuation of a lost battle. We also have to consider those situations in which it is questionable whether there is human life at all.

I have mentioned earlier that it is sometimes hard to say whether a person is still alive. After an accident a patient may be in a deep coma. There can be severe brain damage. The heartbeat may be maintained artificially, but the fact that the heart still works does not prove that the person is alive. In the case of a heart transplant a person's heart continues to work, even in someone else's body. No one will maintain that the heart donor is still alive, because "his" heart is beating. No, he was probably killed in an accident, and someone else received his heart while it was still working or after it had been reactivated.

Also the opposite happens: after a cardiac arrest, when a heart stops, and even when it is replaced, either by another heart or by a heart pump, the person is still alive, but his heart is dead.

The same counts for other organs. So-called life-saving devices can take over the functions of different organs, or keep them going, even after the person has died.

At what time is a doctor allowed to switch off the equipment? In other words: When is a patient dead?

There are situations in which we really can speak of "life-saving devices" and "prolonging life," at least from a human point of view. But there are also situations in which the equipment only maintains the flow of blood, the heartbeat, the oxygen supply, and perhaps some metabolic processes in a dead body.

Where does the borderline lie between life and death? The most commonly accepted indication nowadays seems to be a repeatedly flat EEG, an isoelectric encephalogram. You might wonder what this "technical" term is all about. The brain produces very small electrical pulses. This activity can be registered with an electronic device. That provides a so-called EEG. If the test shows no activity at all, it is called a flat EEG. If such a test, repeatedly performed at certain intervals, does not show any activity of the brain, a patient can be pronounced dead. This lack of brain activity is considered to be an irreversible phenomenon.

If the equipment is turned off then, it is not a matter of euthanasia, although the immediate result is that all the other functions of the body stop as well. However, the patient does not die; his life was already terminated.

There are other cases we should consider. Suppose someone is in a terminal stage, either because of serious illness or because of age. Humanly speaking, the person can only live a few days. Then a complication occurs which under normal conditions could have been corrected by an operation or a rather complicated treatment. What are we supposed to do in such a situation? Do we start an action which might prolong the life of the patient, but which also can be too much for him to take, so that he dies during the operation? Or do we refrain from any treatment, admitting that this is part of the terminal process? The latter seems to be a kind of passive euthanasia — leaving undone something that could have prolonged his life.

I am convinced that in cases like this we have to refrain from intervening. We have to admit that the Lord is at work, bringing human life to an end. We should never try to hasten death, but neither should we in a desperate move try to evade the reality of the process of dying. We do not call this passive euthanasia; it is a matter of respect for the Lord, who rules over life and death. To a certain extent, we acknowledge a person's "right" to live, but we should also acknowledge a person's "right" to die quietly, without medical interference at any cost.

6. Heavy sedation

One other point is the use of heavy sedation. Sometimes people wonder whether the use of heavy sedation can be considered a treatment that comes very close to euthanasia. What is the difference between giving a patient a lethal dose to cause euthanasia, and giving increasing doses of sedatives that might be too much for the patient's heart to take?

In this respect we have to be careful. We are dealing with a very sensitive issue and with people in a very vulnerable situation. That means that we should not unnecessarily hurt another's feelings, but we should not ignore the real possibility of giving in to certain unacceptable wishes and practices of a family which can no longer stand seeing the suffering of a beloved one either.

Therefore we have to be very precise in our formulation. What do we mean by euthanasia? It is an action or treatment undertaken or a decision made with the intention of terminating human life or of hastening death. It has to be clearly distinguished from an action or treatment that might have certain dangerous side effects, but that is intended to give relief or to cure an illness. With every medicine there is the risk of undesired side effects. What risks we can take and what side effects we can accept, depends on the seriousness of the case.

Today there is a tendency to use very strong medicines, and it is doubtful whether this is alway really necessary. Too many drugs are sold over the counter and too many tranquilizers are used today, and the side effects are evident. But when someone has cancer, it can be necessary to use medicines whose side effects in other circumstances are unacceptable. It is the same with sedation in a terminal case. When someone suffers terrible pain, relief can be given and may be given by morphine, although morphine is a very strong medicine. A large dose can become too much for the heart. However, the treatment is given with the intention of relieving the pain, although the side effect, humanly speaking, may be a shortening of life.

In such a case we are not making any decisions about life or death; we are only making a responsible decision concerning the relief that can be given to a person during the last days of his life. We can also put it this way: we do not decide on the length of a person's life, but we try to improve the quality of life within the limits set by the Lord.

7. Telling the truth

Another important point we have to face in cases of terminal illness is the matter of telling the truth. Is a doctor supposed to tell a patient the truth and will he do so? Most people say to the doctor, "Please, tell me the truth." In most cases the doctor is not prepared to tell the patient exactly everything he knows or expects to happen.

When we believe in Jesus Christ our Lord and Saviour, we should be able to face the reality of death, and we need not be fooled or misled by a doctor who gives us false "hope."

The matter is not as easy as it seems, however.

What is "the truth" in this respect? Almost every patient says to the doctor, "Tell me the truth." Even unbelievers say so. But often they only mean: "Please tell me that my illness is not malignant and that it can be cured." When the doctor gives the straight forward reply: "You have only a few months to live," it happens more often than not that the patient becomes upset and says, "Why did you say this? You shouldn't have told me."

That is what the doctor has to consider. He has to be very careful, because he is dealing with human feelings and emotions which are not always reasonable and logical, but nonetheless very real.

With respect to believers it is a different matter, although the physician does not always know whether his patient is a believer and what his faith means to him. If the doctor is not a believer himself, we cannot expect that he understands what faith means in human life.

Besides: what is "the truth" in this respect? A specialist can give his prognosis, but that is always his personal opinion about the course a disease will probably take. It can be considered an expectation of what, in his opinion is going to happen — a more or less reliable expectation. A doctor can never say exactly what the course of a disease will be. There have been many cases where the physician expected a person to die within a couple of weeks or days, while it took more than a year. On the other hand, sometimes it goes much faster than the doctor had expected. There are also cases where a doctor cannot make any prognosis whatsoever about how long a patient still has to live.

Whatever the situation, a physician has to be very careful. He should not bother a patient or make him upset with a too pessimistic prediction. Nor should he give a patient false hope for recovery. Therefore an honest doctor, who is prepared to tell the truth, has to confine himself to explaining what he, with a great degree of probability, expects or knows. As long as he does not have sufficient evidence, he should say nothing; he should not cause unnecessary worry.

There is another aspect we have to consider, and that is the process of acceptance through which the patient and his relatives have to go.

When a fatal illness becomes manifest, the family usually first goes through a period in which they seem to ignore reality. Although they know better, they talk about the possibility of recovery and seem to grasp at every straw to make others and themselves believe that it is not that serious. Later they go through a period when they can speak about it and accept reality. If the patient has to suffer terrible pain, there may even come a time when he longs for the end. But it happens quite often that a terminal patient, on a day when he feels better, speaks about the future as if he really expects a full recovery. We shouldn't call that self-deception or ignoring reality. It is a natural human reaction, also for Christians. The Lord didn't promise to give us courage to die as long as we have a task to live. Death remains an enemy. Christ has taken away the sting of death, but death remains an unnatural thing. A Christian does not long for death. In Philippians 1:23 Paul says that it is his desire to depart and be with Christ. To be with Christ is far better, and that is his desire. That is also our comfort and that can take away the sting of death, but death is still an enemy. We can be assured that the Lord will not forsake His children, not even in the hour of their death. But as long as we are alive, and in good health, it is natural that we desire to stay alive and to do our work. The desire to die is not a healthy attitude; it is not a Christian attitude for healthy people. That brings us to another point.

8. Suicide

Suicide is the act of killing oneself. It is a topic which is often shunned in discussions. A lot of misunderstanding exists in this respect.

The first thing we have to say is that an attempt to commit suicide can ripen only in a sick mind. It is a desperate action of someone who does not see any way out of his problems, and who is not willing or able to fight any longer; he is not even prepared to think about the consequences of his action. It also happens among believers, more often than we are aware of.

When we study this subject, it becomes clear that an attempted suicide is a cry for help and attention from someone who is desperate and not able to continue his fight. It is not always meant as a real attempt to commit suicide, or, at least, the person does not always fully realize the consequences of his action. Many cases are pretended attempts that ran out of control. However, it also happens that people are so sick of mind that they see it as the only way out.

Outsiders are sometimes very cruel in their judgment on someone who commits suicide. They are quick to quote Ecclesiastes 11:3: "In the place where the tree falls, there it will lie," and their exegesis of this text is: his last act was murder, so there was no repentance and consequently no forgiveness. We have heard people saying in a situation like this: "We do not judge; we leave it up to the Lord; but in the place where the tree falls, there it will lie." In this way they did *not* leave it up to the Lord; they have already passed their own judgment, condemning the person.

Of course, suicide is murder. We are not allowed to kill anyone, neither ourselves nor another. But we also know that there is forgiveness for murderers. When Christ died, a murderer was allowed to be with Him in Paradise.

Don't say that in the case of suicide there is no time for repentance. We do not know what happens in someone's mind in the last few moments, when he is no longer able to stop the process that he has set in motion. Furthermore, the judgment of the Lord does not depend on our very last action, either good or bad, and certainly not on the consequences of an action caused or thought up by a sick mind. We should leave the judgment up to the Lord, but that means that we make no judgment at all, neither in a positive nor in a negative way.

At the same time we should try to give help to people who feel so desperate that they are almost ready to commit suicide. In many instances they have problems which bother them, and which they neither can nor will discuss with others. It can be a matter of homosexuality, alcoholism, or anything else. They are afraid to talk with others about their problems; they feel like outcasts and are afraid they will be expelled from society if people will find out about their problems. And in the end they are not able to cope with their problems any longer.

Also among Christians there are hidden alcoholics — not only men but also women, young ladies as well as older people. Also among Christians there are homophiles, more than most people think. The word *homophiles* does not refer to people who practise homosexuality but to those who have different feelings than others. They know that homosexuality is sin, and therefore they do not give in to their desires, but fight their whole life long against their homophilia, always afraid that someone may find out their different attitude and that they may be cast out. Such people sometimes have a terrible inferiority complex. Their feelings of loneliness and desperation can drive them to suicide.

It is beyond the scope of this chapter to go into more detail on this topic. That would require a special chapter. May what has been said so far suffice to show that we should not be too hard and quick with our judgment on people who commit suicide or who attempt to do so. Instead we should try to help them before it comes to this desperate action, and we should pray for them.

9. Organ transplants

There is one more issue which is closely related to the borderline of human life, and that is organ transplants. Are they acceptable for a Christian? Some say that we are not allowed to mutilate our body intentionally by taking away some organs, not even after our death. Others consider it too great an infringement upon the nature of the human body as the LORD created it, to change or replace parts, as with a car.

The first argument is not a very strong one. We have to respect the work of the LORD, also in the way we deal with a dead body. But if we can serve others, or save a life by making a part of our body available for transplant after our death, we do not mutilate our body but rather fulfil the commandment of the LORD in serving others with our body. That counts for helping the blind with our eyes as well as for kidney transplants.

The second argument mentioned above has to be considered as well. Is it too great an infringement upon human life? There is an even more pressing question in this respect, and that is: When does a heart become available for transplant? After the donor has died, of course. But when the heart has been silent for too long, it cannot be used for transplant purposes any longer. It should be taken away while it is still beating. The patient who is waiting for a transplant needs a healthy, beating heart without any damage. But as long as a patient is alive, his heart cannot be taken away; that would kill him instantly. Determining the exact moment of death becomes very critical. Taking away the heart of the donor too early means murder; taking it away too late makes the heart useless for transplantation. Even the previously mentioned method of a flat EEG is not sufficient in this respect: it takes too much time. The only way to get a heart for transplantation is to wait for a patient who is so seriously injured in a car accident that, although his heart is still beating, he cannot survive (e.g. because his head is crushed). It is clear that in such a case decisions have to be made quickly and that we have to face the risk that there are conflicting interests in pronouncing someone dead. Therefore it is a strict condition that the physician who pronounces the patient dead is in no way involved in or related to the team that performs the heart transplant.

All this makes heart transplants a precarious matter. Nowadays we hear futurists speak about brain transplants. They say that, technically speaking, it is possible, but the technology of the operation has to be further developed, especially with respect to microsurgery. We don't know whether such an operation will ever be performed. It is, however, perfectly clear that the points we have mentioned above with respect to heart transplants count even more with respect to brain transplants.

If this should ever become possible, we will have to consider the ethical implications. Who is who? Does a patient receive another brain? Or is someone's personality located in his brain, so that the donor of the brain basically lives further in another body? Which person is alive?

If this trend continues, we may reach the point where — as someone predicted — they will put together two severely injured people, making one survivor out of them. We will come back to this issue and its implications in another chapter.

We don't know what will happen in the future. It is important to be on the alert. Human beings will be able to perform almost unbelievable things. They will try to gain control over every form of human life, to manipulate it, to bring forth life, and to get rid of it, just as they please.

But we know and confess: human life is created by the Lord our God. He is the only One who decides on the beginning of it, and He is also the One who has the right to bring life to an end.

We trust in Him our God. Whatever human beings may do, our God and Father has everything in His hand. Under His protection we are safe. We don't have to worry, even when we reach the borderline of human life. His Sovereign government extends over this borderline, because we are Christ's own in life and death, for ever.

CHAPTER EIGHT

Test-tube Babies

1. A Brave New World?

In 1932 Aldous Huxley published his fantasy of the future. In this novel he describes in science-fiction fashion how human beings are "produced" in the "Central London Hatchery and Conditioning Centre." Marriage, family life, and pregnancy have become things of the past. In a huge and medically clean laboratory human eggs are fertilized and are "raised," in bottles until they have been "grown" to "perfectly formed embryos." During this growing process they are "conditioned" in such a way that the "produced" human beings fit exactly the requirements set by the "World Controler."

They "produce" basically five "classes" of human beings, the so-called Alphas, Betas, Gammas, Deltas, and Epsilons. The Alphas are the most excellent, intelligent scientists, while the Epsilons are the lowest class of human beings, having no intelligence. They are "predestined" to do only simple physical work.

During the growing process all embryos are "conditioned" in such a way that they, physically as well as mentally, fit the task for which they are "produced." The "lower class" people have fewer desires; everyone is perfectly happy and satisfied with his own situation and his own task. Social stability is maintained, because no one has any desire to take over someone else's place or change his own circumstances. There is no such thing as labour conflict any longer. The lower class individuals, like the Deltas, the Gammas, and the Epsilons, are "produced" in identical series or batches, according to a so-called "bokanovskification" procedure. That means that from one egg not only an identical set of twins can be developed but up to 96 identical persons. In this way they can provide a work-place or a factory with "identical" workers who will never cause any problems among each other.

Some groups of people are "conditioned" to work in an extremely hot environment; others can stand extreme cold. In short, they "produce" all kinds of people exactly according to the customer's specifications, just as nowadays equipment for a factory is developed.

This policy seems to create a completely new society with perfect happiness. Everyone is satisfied with his own circumstances. It is called the "Brave New World" in which human life comes out of a bottle. The favorite song of the children "grown" in these bottles is:

Bottle of mine, it's you I have always wanted!
Bottle of mine, why was I ever decanted?
  Skies are blue inside of you,
  The weather's always fine;
For there ain't no Bottle in all the world
Like that dear little Bottle of mine.

It is a terrible story. Finally, the author shows the vanity also of this seemingly perfect society. When people feel less satisfied they have to take a "pill" to have a "holiday" in a dream of perfect happiness. Especially the "lower class" people find their "entertainment" in such drug-induced dreams. Although the author shows, in a rather sarcastic way, the vanity of this "Brave New World," he does not see the real purpose of human life, namely that we are created as God's image and as His ambassadors in this world, and that our aim and purpose is and always has to be to glorify Him in our whole life.

You may be wondering why I am referring to this book at all. It is certainly not to encourage you to read it. It is rather to show the tremendous impact this book has had and still has upon the way modern scientists think. The book has been reprinted many times, sometimes twice a year. The expression *test-tube baby* which is common today, finds its origin in this book.

At the time this book was printed for the first time, most people did not pay too much attention to it. It was considered to be "science fiction" — more fiction than science, for that matter. However, we seem to have arrived at a point where it is becoming reality. How close are we to such a "Hatchery and Conditioning Centre" in which human eggs are fertilized and "hatched" in an artificial way?

In this chapter we will take note of recent biochemical developments and then try to determine our Christian point of view and approach to these matters.

2. Science fiction or reality?

I will first mention a number of remarkable facts which have recently made world news.

In Australia a couple had tried to receive a "test-tube baby." During the so-called "in vitro fertilization," some eggs were fertilized and one of them was implanted in the mother's womb, but this led to a miscarriage. Some other fertilized eggs were "frozen" and, in this way, "stored" for a possible next attempt. However, the couple died in a traffic accident, and now physicians and lawyers are fighting about the question whether the fertilized eggs are "persons." The couple left behind an estate worth millions. Many women have offered to serve as "surrogate mothers" to bear a fertilized egg to delivery and claim the child as heir of the estate.

In France a man had to undergo a treatment that would make him sterile. Before the surgery, some of his sperm was "frozen" and kept in a laboratory. Later this man got married and shortly after the marriage he died. His widow asked to be artificially inseminated with his sperm in order as yet to receive a child by her former husband, although the sperm was "frozen" before they got married. Her claim was denied by the doctors, but a court granted her request.

In the past, artificial insemination was something only practiced on animals. Nowadays, not only "Artificial Insemination with the sperm of the woman's own Husband" (A.I.H.) but also "Artificial Insemination with sperm of an anonymous Donor" (A.I.D.) is common practice in most countries. According to statistics, every year about 10,000 women in the U.S.A. receive a child via A.I.D.

Apart from the problems mentioned above, we are confronted with cases of "surrogate motherhood." Couples who cannot receive children in the normal way can use a "surrogate mother" to have "their" child implanted in the womb of a "hired" person. Some women are willing to make money in this way, and there are couples who are willing to pay a lot of money for such "services." However, these practices have far-reaching consequences. I have already mentioned the legal problems which have served in court cases. There are legal questions such as "Who is the heir of the estate?" and "Who is the owner of the frozen eggs or the sperm?" We are not interested in the first place in these legal matters, but rather in what the Word of God teaches us about human life and the origin of it. Are we allowed to use or to be involved in these sorts of things?

Before we determine our attitude and approach, we should first have a closer look at what it is really all about, because much confusion and many misconceptions seem to exist as to what a "test-tube baby" is. The name is misleading, because no test-tube is used. The name "test-tube baby" is, more or less, from Aldous Huxley's novel. The proper name is "In Vitro Fertilization," and from now on we will refer to it as I.V.F.

3. In vitro fertilization

What is I.V.F. all about? Without going into too much medical detail, I will try to explain what happens. As a rule every month one egg leaves a woman's ovary and moves slowly via one of the fallopian tubes to the womb. If, on its way, the egg meets sperm, one spermatozoon may penetrate the egg. If that happens, the egg is "fertilized," and no other spermatozoon can penetrate it. We call this "conception." It means that a new human being has been created, intricately wrought by the LORD, as Psalm 139 says. The fertilized egg moves on into the womb, where it imbeds itself in the wall of the uterus to develop in about nine months into a full-grown baby. That is the "normal" process of conception and birth.

I.V.F. means that some eggs are surgically removed from a woman's body and brought together with sperm in a glass dish, in an attempt to fertilize the eggs. (The expression in vitro means literally "in glass.") After a number of days one of the fertilized eggs in implanted into the woman's womb, to develop there in the normal way. The reason for such an operation is often a blockage of the fallopian tubes. The egg cannot reach the womb to be fertilized in the normal way.

So far there seems to be nothing wrong with the procedure. It is just another operation to overcome a physical obstacle in a woman's body. It is sometimes compared with artificial insemination, in which the sperm of a woman's husband is placed in the woman's womb with medical instruments, because a physical defect prevents it from getting there in the "normal" way. Apart from the objections which we may have even to such artificial insemination, there is a great difference between A.I.H. and I.V.F. In the first place, there is the fact that conception takes place outside the human body. The question has to be asked whether or not that is too much of an intrusion into the natural process of conception, described in Psalm 139 as "intricately wrought" by the LORD Himself.

Besides, with I.V.F. often more than one egg is fertilized. The doctor has to make a choice: he must pick the "best" of them to implant into the womb and destroy the others. However, since we believe that after conception we are dealing with human beings, it would mean the destruction of human life — a form of murder.

Although I realize that the modern I.V.F. is a far cry from the test-tube babies described in Huxley's book, it is too much of an intrusion into God's creation of new life to be acceptable for believers. If we accept this kind of manipulation, we are on a dangerous and slippery slope. Recent publications show us how close we have come to the development and the manipulation of human life described in Huxley's novel.

4. Alarming developments

To show how dangerous and alarming the present developments are, I will pass on some information found it in *Right to Life NEWS*, the magazine of the "Right to Life Association of Toronto and Area."

The Karolinska research hospital in Stockholm is one of the most renowned hospitals in Europe. I have had the privilege to visit this hospital a few times for study purposes. Dr. Largs Hamberger is one of the specialists associated with this hospital. According to Dr. Hamberger, researchers are already using human sperm to fertilize animal eggs "in vitro." The European Medical Research Association has approved such experiments, according to Dr. Hamberger. They are using hamster ova, and rat and mice eggs, and they have approved, in principle, the fertilization of monkey ova with human sperm. It is little consolation to read that the embryos "are not allowed to develop past initial cell cleavage stage in test tubes." This only means that for the time being the results of such experiments are destroyed in an early stage, to prevent the development of "monstrous" creatures.

Dr. Hamberger says: "I am personally a little scared at the experiments and I am very surprised that there has not been a wider public reaction for discussion on the topic . . . . Whichever way you look at it, you end up with ethical problems . . . . To my knowledge, no one has yet carried out the experiment on the higher species of ape, but one can have one's thoughts that some researcher may try it."

Dr. Hamberger was one of twelve experts in human and animal genetics called before the European Medical Advisory Council in Brussels last June, when the council established guidelines. The recommendations state: "Studies on interspecies interactions involving human gametes are valuable in providing information on the penetrating capacity and chromosomal complement of sperm. The product, however, should not be allowed to develop beyond the early cleavage stages." (Quote from *Right to Life NEWS*, June 1984.)

This is an alarming development, and, with Dr. Hamberger, I am surprised that there has not been a wider public reaction. It is about time that we become aware of what is going on in this respect. I.V.F. is presented as an innocent procedure, just another medical treatment to help couples who cannot receive children in the normal way. In the last six years, 500 "test-tube babies" have been born in England. Let us be on the alert. We have to see it as part of a development in which biochemists are trying to take the origin of human life into their own hands.

The two main reasons why we reject the use of I.V.F. are, in the first place, that the conception of human life becomes a matter of biochemical manipulation, and, in the second place, that during this process the doctor has to make a choice which fertilized egg will be implanted into the womb. If we consider conception to be the beginning of human life, then this choice involves a decision regarding which human being will be given an opportunity to grow to normal life, which ones will be destroyed, and which ones may be "frozen" to be used in a next experiment.

An additional reason is the following. Dr. Donald De Marco, who is with the faculty of philosophy at St. Jerome's College, University of Waterloo, said at a recent public meeting that many researchers require the parents to permit abortion should deformities be suspected.

Acceptance of I.V.F. inevitably places us in the position of getting involved in abortion and other deliberate killings of human beings, either in the mother's womb or already before they have reached this natural environment. We have come closer to Huxley's science fiction story than many of us may be aware of.

5. Artificial insemination

After what has been said in previous sections, a few remarks have to be made about artificial insemination. It is clear that we reject every form of A.I.D., in which sperm from an anonymous donor is used. This is simply a violation of the unity between husband and wife and of the holy married state. It boils down to adultery in a medical, technical way. If A.I.D. is acceptable, no one should be surprised if the next step were the acceptance of physical adultery to help a couple that wants to have a baby. The LORD has instituted the married state and the unity of husband and wife, and He wants to use this unity to continue and increase the human race, as we can read in the Form for the Solemnization of Marriage. Also in this respect, the warning holds true that what God has joined together, man should not put asunder.

It is a different story with A.I.H. Then the unity between husband and wife in the married state is honoured. Husband and wife are the natural parents of the child conceived in such a way. Sometimes it is argued that the procreation of a child is disconnected from the union between husband and wife in which they become "one flesh." Allegedly it is disconnected from the sexual union. However, that is not necessarily so. A.I.H. is not meant to replace the sexual union between husband and wife; at least it should not be used in that way. It does happen that a physical defect prevents a woman from becoming pregnant. In such a case A.I.H. can help to overcome such an obstacle. The fact that this medical procedure is not "natural" does not make it unacceptable per se. Many children are born by Caesarean section, and that is not the "natural way" either, but still it is generally accepted. The decisive criteria in this matter are, in the first place, that conception takes place in the normal way in the body of the mother, and, in the second place, that the child is a child of husband and wife, a child that grows in the normal way in the womb of the mother.

This is not the case with A.I.D. and I.V.F. because, with the former, the child is not a child of the husband, while, with the latter, conception takes place outside the body of the mother and some "human beings" are simply destroyed after the researcher has made his choice on the basis of "quality."

For these reasons I believe that in certain circumstances A.I.H. can be an acceptable procedure to overcome a medical and physical obstacle, while both A.I.D. and I.V.F. are unacceptable in any circumstances.

6. Final remarks

These matters have far-reaching moral and ethical implications; further consideration is necessary. I hope that in this chapter some food for thought has been given. We are living in a world in which respect for human life is rapidly declining. Talking about human rights, about constitutional rights and freedoms, does not really help as long as people do not respect the Rights of the LORD God Almighty, the Creator of human life.

Psalm 139 speaks in a beautiful and impressive way about human life and the origin of human life, especially in verses 13-18:

"For Thou didst form my inward parts,
 Thou didst knit me together in my mother's womb.
I praise Thee, for Thou art fearful and wonderful.
 Wonderful are Thy works!
Thou knowest me right well;
 my frame was not hidden from Thee,
when I was being made in secret,
 intricately wrought in the depths of the earth.

Thy eyes beheld my unformed substance;
in Thy book were written, every one of them,
the days that were formed for me,
when as yet there was none of them.
How precious to me are Thy thoughts, O God!
How vast is the sum of them!
If I would count them, they are more than the sand.
When I awake, I am still with Thee."

This is a song of praise to the glory of God, our Creator. Let that be our confession and the guideline for our discussions about these matters. And let us not forget what follows in verses 19-24:

"O that Thou wouldst slay the wicked, O God,
and that the men of blood would depart from me,
men who maliciously defy Thee,
who lift themselves up against Thee for evil!
Do I not hate them that hate Thee, O LORD?
And do I not loathe them that rise up against Thee?
I hate them with perfect hatred;
I count them my enemies.
Search me, O God, and know my heart!
Try me and know my thoughts!
And see if there be any wicked way in me,
and lead me in the way everlasting!"

That is a strong warning to be on the alert and to resist and fight all those who try to destroy the wonder of God's creating power or to intrude on His intricate work.

It also contains a warning to examine our own hearts, to see "if there is any wicked way in us."

May the LORD, by His Holy Spirit, "lead us in the way everlasting."

CHAPTER NINE

Organ Transplants

1. Baby Fae

A two-week-old baby in the U.S.A. made world news. In a hospital in Loma Linda, in California, U.S.A., a baby was born with an incurable heart defect. Humanly speaking the baby had only a few weeks to live. The only cure was a heart transplant. In five hours of surgery the heart of a seven-month-old baboon was implanted into the body of the two-week-old baby. The real name of the baby has not been released, but the baby is known everywhere as Baby Fae.

This surgery has caused a lot of discussion. Some are protesting against it, while others are in favour of it and are very excited. It is considered a big step in a new direction, since it opens new avenues for the transplantation of animal organs into human beings.

Let's analyze the arguments of those who are in favour of this operation as well as of those who are against it.

We will first take a look at the reasoning of some protesters.

2. Cruelty to animals?

Some have protested against this operation because they consider it cruel to kill a healthy baboon just to prolong the suffering of a child. Their reasoning is that the child was bound to die anyway, because the human body rejects animal tissue, and consequently two die: the baby and the baboon.

This is not a valid objection. The question whether the baby ultimately survived is irrelevant. Even if the life of a baby can be prolonged only for a short period of time, it still might be sufficient reason to try. The real point is whether the life of an animal may be sacrificed for the sake of a human being. We believe that God has given man dominion over all creatures. That includes the right to kill animals to serve mankind. We are not allowed to be cruel to animals and to let them suffer unnecessarily, but we are allowed to kill animals — not only to save or prolong human life, but even to enjoy a good meal. The Bible teaches us clearly that the life of an animal is not sacred or on the same level as human life. In order to organize a party or to have a festive meal, the fatted calf was killed. I cannot see anything wrong with killing an animal for this purpose, especially not when it is done without causing any suffering or pain. Some experiments with animals may be cruel, especially when an animal is made sick to find out the reaction to a certain drug or to poison. Such suffering should be avoided as much as possible. But there is nothing wrong with killing an animal as such.

3. Foreign tissue

In the discussions about Baby Fae, we heard the argument that no human heart was available. Some argue that the heart of a two-year-old child was available. Others say that this would not have served the purpose, because it was too big for a two-week-old baby. It was also argued that the human heart became available at a moment when the transplant procedure had been started already and was too far underway to change to another heart. Although this might seem to be a valid reason, it really is irrelevant. If it is correct and acceptable to use an animal organ, it does not really matter whether there is another heart available. The only point, then, is which one suits the purpose better.

Also the matter of rejection of foreign tissue was brought up. It is a generally known fact that the human body tends to reject any foreign object which enters the body. That counts for a sliver in your finger as well as for a blood transfusion or an organ transplant. The body's attempt to get rid of foreign objects is a natural reaction to protect itself. These reaction symptoms can be avoided if the body does not recognize the object as being "foreign." Therefore it is necessary to choose a donor for blood transfusion purposes carefully, to ensure that the blood is similar to the blood of the patient. That determines the choice of material for artificial organs, a plastic hip or a steel pin in a broken leg. It also determines the choice of a donor for a heart transplant. The more similar the tissue of the donor is to that of the recipient, the less chance there is that the body will reject the organ as a "foreign object." Another way to avoid the rejection symptoms is to eliminate or lower the defence system of the body. That is done to a certain extent during and after every heart transplant. However, this brings with it the risk of all kinds of infections, because the body loses its natural defences against these intruders as well.

Up till now, the transplantation of an animal heart was never successfully performed because of this rejection phenomenon. The animal tissue is too "foreign" to be accepted anyway. With a newborn baby the defence system is not fully developed. That is why this operation on a two-week-old-baby could be performed. However, the baby survived for only three weeks.

4. The real point at stake

What is the real point in this matter? In my opinion, it is the ethical question whether we are allowed to transplant organs from an animal into a human being. Of similar importance is the question what attitude is behind this whole development. Some argue that the use of animal tissue in an operation is a long-standing practice — heart valves of pigs have been successfully implanted into human beings for many years. The bowels of cats are used to prepare the material for stitches which cannot be reached to remove after an operation and which therefore have to dissolve. However, apart from the objection one might have even against these practices, in all these instances we were dealing with minor "parts" and not with the transplantation of vital organs.

I do not agree with the reasoning that the heart is the center of spiritual life and that therefore a heart transplant is forbidden in all circumstances. When the Bible says that we have to serve the LORD with all our heart and that from the heart are the springs of life, the Bible does not refer, in the first place, to the physical organ that functions as a blood pump, but to the spiritual center of our existence and our personality. And yet, the heart is so vital an organ that a heart transplant is about as far as we can go in organ transplantation.

The philosophy behind all this is also important. Doctors are talking about interspecies transplants. By the expression *interspecies* they mean: between the different species of animals. They first tried it between dog and wolf. Now they will try it between ape and man. They consider mankind to be the most highly developed animal. One of the doctors who performed the operation stated that he loves animals, but, as a member of the human species of animals, he prefers to help a human being at the cost of a baboon.

The LORD has made man His ambassador, created after His image, to have dominion over all creatures, also over the animals. We are allowed to use animals for food and to work for us. But we should not consider human life as just a higher form of animal life. Our main objection to interspecies transplants is that it does not recognize the principle difference between man and animal. It shows a lack of respect for God, the Creator of human life, and a lack of recognition of the fact that human life is very unique. Here we find the same attitude as with the experiments with in vitro fertilization, mentioned in the previous chapter. It is part of an effort to manipulate human life and to demonstrate that human beings are in control of everything, independent of God — or even *instead of* God, the Creator of human life.

5. Organ transplants in general

Some remarks about organ transplants in general. I mentioned already that, although our physical heart is not the center of our spiritual life, heart transplantation is about as far as we can go with respect to organ transplants. We have to be aware of what is going on in this field. From recent publications we can learn that microsurgery has opened completely new avenues. Microsurgery is a technique of working with stitches which are invisible to the naked human eye. Only with a magnifying glass or microscope can they be seen. This technique has made it possible to transplant even an ovary and a fallopian tube from one woman to another. Because of the rejection mechanism mentioned before, this operation has been performed successfully only with identical twins. Still it may become possible in the future to cure infertility in this way. However, the question remains: Are we allowed to use such procedures? The main problem is: Who is who? Who is the "mother" when a child is born after such an operation. Is it the *donor* of the ovary and fallopian tube or is it the *recipient* of these organs? Because we are dealing with the organs of procreation, which determine the personality and the character of the human being to be brought forth, we are intruding too much into God's work of creation of human life. We have arrived at the same slippery slope as with artificial insemination with the sperm of a donor.

The same problem of personality changes arises when we think about transplanting a human brain or parts of it. That is impossible at the present time for technical reasons. With the more sophisticated technology of microsurgery, it may become possible in the future.

We Christians confess that human life comes from the hand of the Lord. In modern medical developments, the Lord has given us wonderful means to cure illness and to relieve pain. However, we have to realize that there are limits. We have to show our respect for the majesty of our Creator in abiding by these limits.

Continuous study of the ethical aspects of this subject is necessary. Let us help one another to find the right, Christian approach in these matters.

CHAPTER TEN

Child Abuse

1. Some statistics

Child abuse and child molestation are issues not too frequently discussed among Christians. Most of us seem to think that these things do not happen in our circles. It may be a danger which threatens our youngsters when they travel or when they go to dark, dirty places, but such things do not happen in the secure and protective environment of a Christian family or a Christian society!

However, this notion is not correct. Recently many cases have hit the news. That does not necessarily mean that this phenomenon is on the increase. It can also be that people are speaking more openly about it. Especially the victims have more opportunities to ask for help, to explain and discuss their problems with people who are willing to listen and to help.

Child abuse and molestation is not something that is restricted to the social lower class or to the "outcast." It happens among all kinds of people, even in the upper echalons of society. It also happens among Christians.

Recent publications have given us a grim picture of the reality of this fact. Among the people who have been convicted we find doctors, teachers, company directors, and other highly respected people. Many of them are financially well off, generally known as nice, well-behaving people and sometimes fathers of respectable families.

According to statistics, one out of five American children has been molested in one way or another before reaching the age of 18 years; 90% of them are molested not by strangers but by good friends of the family or by members of the family. Most victims are molested in their own home.

These things do happen also among Christians. Although most cases will never come into the open, there is a lot of suffering because of such molestation. Children suffer the most because they cannot, or do not dare to, talk about it with anybody. Statistics show that parents, as well as pastors, teachers, and church officials, have been convicted of child molestation. According to some experts, it seems that well-behaving and well-educated children are even more prone to becoming victims. They say that "good kids" especially are a rewarding target for child abusers. You may wonder why. I will try to explain this in the next section.

2. Who are the victims?

A police officer, in charge of investigations in such crimes, pointed to some very interesting and remarkable facts. Children in a Christian family are taught to respect and obey adults. They are not supposed to "talk back." Younger children have the impression that what adults do, say or ask must be right, especially when they are highly respected persons. Now, this may be a proper attitude for children, but it also makes them more vulnerable as victims of molestation. These children have a highly developed sense of the code of honour: You are not allowed to break your promise. They can be put under pressure. The molester tells them that he knows what he is doing and that they are not allowed to tell anyone about these things. They are forced to promise that they will never talk about it to others. And then they feel obliged to keep their promise. That makes well-educated and well-behaved children an easier target for child molesters.

There are some other aspects which have to be considered. A molester always looks for someone who for one reason or another is "different" from the rest, and who therefore feels lonely, rejected, left out, or, at least, not completely accepted in his group of peers. Sometimes they are children who do not receive the love and affection they need and who are therefore eager to accept a relationship which offers them special attention and something they feel as love and affection.

Other frequent targets are physically precocious children, who for that reason do not feel at ease among their peers. They look older than they are, although they mentally still need contact with children of their own age. The older children do not accept them because of their age, and the younger ones do not see them as their equals because of the way they look and do not fully accept them for that reason. The molester knows exactly how to exploit these feelings. He offers the comfort, the affection, and the personal relationship they are missing and looking for. Such children are sometimes willing to endure the suffering, the physical harm, and the stress, in order to maintain the relationship and to receive the attention from someone who seems to care for them. They may even protect their molester, rather than try to escape his attack.

3. Who is the offender?

Some people seem to think that a child molester is a "bad looking guy" whom you can recognize right away by the way he looks at you, by the way he is dressed, behaves, and talks. However, this picture is not correct. They are often well-behaving, highly respected persons. Among those who have been convicted we find babysitters, teachers, fathers, grandfathers, and other relatives.

In most cases no one is aware of or suspects the relationship. That makes it even more dangerous. Often when a child tries to talk about it or refers to it, he or she is not believed or taken seriously.

Another problem is that children often cannot escape the relationship. When they are abused by their father or by a brother, they usually are terribly frightened, but they feel they have to live with their "secret" because they have a place in the family. If they were to divulge the matter, they would probably get caught up in a tight squeeze. It could create a situation which is even more embarrassing for them than the actual abuse is. That is why so many children who are victims of molestation live with their "secret." They do not dare to speak about it; they are afraid to divulge the matter and bring the relationship to an end until it is already too late. The relationship may come to an end when they reach maturity. But still the frustration lasts and the damage is done. We have seen too many people who never got rid of their frustrations, not even when they had talked it out at a later time. Let us not underestimate the physical as well as the psychological damage that has been done. It happens quite often that problems arise in their own marriage because they have a completely wrong conception of what a real sexual relation is all about. When a minister or other counselor is confronted with marriage problems, quite often the origin appears to be molestation of one of the partners during childhood. It is not the exception that a family member, either one of the parents, or one of the brothers or sisters, a grandfather or another close relative or friend, is the perpetrator. It is extremely difficult to remove misconceptions and frustrations which have built up over many years, even from childhood to parenthood.

4. How to prevent child abuse

After what has been said in the previous sections, parents may wonder how they can prevent such things from happening. We have seen already that children are taught to respect and obey adults and to submit to the authorities. That can make children more likely to become victims. However, we would be putting the cart before the horse if we would try to avoid child abuse by teaching our children to disobey and reject the authority of adults. What we must do is teach them that there are limits to obedience. We also have to teach them that they have to keep their promises, but that there are promises which never should be made and therefore, if made, should not be kept. An important general rule which parents have to instil in their children is: if someone asks you *not* to talk about something and never to tell your father *and* your mother about it, it is probably wrong and therefore you *should* tell both of your parents.

Another thing is that parents have to talk openly and frankly with their children about sexual matters. That does not mean that they have to discuss all kind of details which are not yet at the level of their children's comprehension. Neither does it mean a lack of respect for very intimate issues. On the contrary. It means that children have to know that they can always discuss with their parents anything that bothers them. The more openly parents speak with their children, the less a molester will be able to speculate on the curiosity of the children and their eagerness to get involved in "secret" matters.

Parents should not scare their children with all kinds of vague warnings about possible molesters or bad people. That can make them afraid of and uneasy with everyone outside of the family circle. Parents should be as specific as possible. Very young children do not understand the real meaning of these things. Still they have to be warned. The best way is to teach them to say no if anyone tries to touch them in such a way that they feel uncomfortable. If that happens they should tell their parents about it. A general bit of advice which specialists in the field of child abuse give is to tell children to say no, and to yell and to scream if anyone tries to touch them in the area that their bathing suits would cover. Such incidents should always be reported to *both* parents.

Another point is that parents should be aware of the fact that they have to *listen* to their children. When police officers or counselors are confronted with such cases, they often ask, "Why did you never talk about it with your parents?" Too often the answer is: "I have tried once (or a few times), but they were too busy, and they did not understand what I was talking about or referring to." We should realize that it is not easy for a child to start talking about such things, and when parents, by their attitude, signal to their child: "Don't bother me; I am too busy with other things," the child will be very hesitant to try it again and will keep the matter to himself as a "secret," with all the devastating consequences.

We are living in a time in which people talk openly and freely about sexuality. Most of the time their discussions display a lack of respect for sexuality as a gift of the Lord in human life. We do not correct this situation by avoiding conversations on this topic in our family life. It should not be considered "dirty." On the contrary. It is in the family that children should learn to have respect for and to talk respectfully about sexual life. If they know that they can talk about it openly with their parents, they will be less vulnerable and less prone to becoming a victim of child molestation.

Nowadays we hear about all kinds of civic actions and action centers, about child abuse clinics and emergency centers, to assist, advise and counsel victims. Sometimes it may be necessary to ask for professional help and counseling to prevent lasting psychological and physical harm. However, this help should come from the parents in the first place. Professional help should, if at all possible, be given in close cooperation and at the request of the parents.

There are exceptions. When the parents themselves are the perpetrators of the molestation, intervention by the civil government, either via the Ministry of Human Resources or via the Ministry of Justice, may be necessary. However, also in this respect it is true that an ounce of prevention is better than a pound of cure. Parents, be on the alert!

P.S. Some of the information for this chapter has been gleaned from *Focus on the Family*, November 1984.

CHAPTER ELEVEN

Capital Punishment

1. What are the motives?

Recently, dealing with the sixth commandment, I asked the students in a catechism class to write an essay on capital punishment. I asked this, *before* I had given my opinion. In this way I could find out what their spontaneous responses were, and I elaborated on the subject after I had read the submissions.

It was interesting to notice that they were unanimously in favour of reinstating capital punishment. Different points of view were brought to the fore. Some very strong and Scriptural grounds were mentioned, but also less pure and un-Biblical motives were given. In this chapter I will use the information gathered in this way to emphasize some aspects which may be forgotten or neglected once in a while, and to warn against some unsound arguments which may be used, probably with good intentions, but which nevertheless are not in harmony with what the Bible teaches us.

Some points *against* capital punishment were raised, which are worth considering. Although they are not decisive, they may give you an idea of the difficulty and the danger involved in this matter.

Some points were brought forward in *favour* of reinstating this sentence. These arguments were not all pure either. They show another aspect we have to be aware of, and that is the danger that we are striving for capital punishment on the ground of un-Scriptural arguments.

As a third category I will mention some aspects which are not decisive in this respect either, but which have to be considered with regard to punishment and corrective measures in general, in order to allow us to come to a balanced judgment.

2. Arguments against capital punishment

First I will mention a number of arguments raised against capital punishment. I will just list them for the time being. Later in this chapter we will evaluate them.

a. *It is not corrective, but rather revengeful.*

The most common motive against capital punishment is that every form of punishment should be corrective, remedial, and restorative — not revengeful. Punishment should be administered, either to restore the damage by paying back in a reasonable way and by making up for the damage done by the offence, or to correct the offender by bringing him to terms with and convincing him of the terrible character of his deeds. It may even be applied to prevent him from commiting the offence again or to protect his potential victims from being exposed to the same violence.

However (these people say), what purpose does capital punishment serve? It does not pay back anything to the victim. It does not restore or remedy any relationship. It does not correct the criminal. It can only give a certain feeling of satisfaction to the victim, but (they say) that should never be the motive of our judicial system.

b. *It does not prevent murder.*

Another argument we often hear for the abolition of capital punishment is that it does not prevent murder. A murderer is often not in a mood to use reasonable considerations. He does not realize or think about the consequences of his deeds. Only rarely, if ever, will the knowledge that he may be sentenced to death prevent him from committing his crime. Therefore (people say) capital punishment does not serve any purpose as far as crime prevention is concerned. It only forces people to plead "not guilty," making it harder for the judicial system to work properly. Who would plead "guilty" when he knows that it means the end for him, because he will be put to death? He has nothing to lose.

c. *It is a final, irrevocable measure.*

A third reason adduced against capital punishment is that it eliminates the possibility of correcting judicial errors. It happens once in a while that someone is convicted although innocent. Since every murderer pleads "not guilty," because he has nothing to lose, it becomes very difficult to produce sufficient evidence to prove his guilt and the chance increases that an innocent person is convicted and sentenced. If the judges later find out that it was a mistake, the penalty cannot be revoked and nothing can be restored. Because of the irrevocable nature of capital punishment, many people are of the opinion that we are never allowed to use it.

d. *It is cruel and inhuman.*

That it is cruel and inhuman is another argument we hear against capital punishment. We are living in an era in which corporal punishment ought to be abolished (they say). We no longer use corporal punishment in our schools, many parents have done away with it and we don't use it in our judicial system any longer, as was the case in the Middle Ages. How can we use the most cruel and far-reaching corporal punishment of the death penalty? Besides, the way people are put to death, e.g. in the electric chair, is so cruel that even reading a story about it makes one sick. To use this method is considered to be in conflict with human dignity and the respect for human life.

e. *We are not allowed to kill.*

Some argue that we simply are not allowed to kill. No one has the right to take away someone else's life. This argument is not only brought forward by people who think in terms of "human rights" but it can also be heard from people who base their reasoning on what the Word of God teaches us. They say that in the Old Testament the death penalty may have been an acceptable tool of justice, but in the New Testament we should do away with it. We have to love our neighbour as ourselves; we have to forgive, we have to show mercy and kindness, even to our enemies. Capital punishment, according to them, contradicts the teaching of Holy Scripture in the New Testament.

f. *There is no possibility of repentance.*

Another argument which we hear quite often is that capital punishment takes away every possibility of repentance. As long as a sinner is alive, he can repent. Especially with criminals who have hardened themselves in sin and who have committed terrible deeds, we should deal in a Christian way, giving them the opportunity to amend their lives, to show repentance, and to start all over again with a life of new obedience to the Lord. Capital punishment, humanly speaking, takes away the time and opportunity for repentance.

So far the arguments against capital punishment. They form quite a list. They sound impressive and for some they may be convincing. In the next section I will try to evaluate these arguments, and then we will see that they are not as solid and convincing as they may at first appear.

3. Evaluation of the arguments

In the previous section the arguments against capital punishment were categorized as follows:

a. It is not corrective, but revengeful.

b. It does not prevent murder.

c. It is a final, irrevocable measure.

d. It is cruel and inhuman.

e. We are not allowed to kill.

f. There is no possibility of repentance.

What is the value and the real weight of these arguments? I will try to evaluate them in the light of what the Word of God teaches us about our responsibility as human beings. We will also consider the emotional aspects and the implications for our human society.

Let us trace them successively.

a. *Is it not corrective, but revengeful?*

The argument is that every punishment should be corrective, remedial, and restorative, not revengeful. It seems that capital punishment does not serve that purpose. At best it gives the victims some satisfaction as a form of revenge, but that should never be the motive for justice.

However, that can be and is actually said about most forms of punishment nowadays. A jail term does not restore the damage done by the victim either. And most people consider it very doubtful whether an extended jail term has a corrective and remedial effect on the murderer. His frustration and his hatred towards society may very well increase during an imprisonment, and the convict may be set free in a very desperate mood after he has finished his term. Therefore, the argument that capital punishment does not cure the criminal nor pay back the damage, is not specific for this case, but can be adduced against almost every form of punishment.

b. *Does it not prevent murder?*

The reasoning that capital punishment does not prevent murder is hard to prove. Of course, in those countries where this sentence is used, murder still exists. But it is difficult to establish how many cases of murder have been prevented by the danger of being caught and sentenced to death. Moreover, the same reasoning can be used with respect to every crime and every punishment.

However, I believe that punishment always has a deterrent effect, at least for the majority of people. Most people will agree that in the United Kingdom capital punishment for the killing of a police officer has worked quite effectively in protecting police officers, even while they did not carry firearms.

Although there is a tendency these days to do away with punishment and retaliation as a deterrent, it is certainly not a strong argument against capital punishment.

c. *Is it a final and irrevocable measure?*

The death penalty is certainly a final and irrevocable measure, and it is not inconceivable that people may be killed by a judicial error.

However, there are at least three aspects we have to consider in this respect.

One: It is highly unlikely in our modern judicial system that someone would be convicted without conclusive evidence. The tendency to give the defendent the benefit of the doubt at the cost of the victims is more prevalent. Especially where capital punishment is involved, special precautions have to be taken to prevent such judicial errors as much as possible.

Two: When someone is sentenced to life imprisonment and his innocence is proven after many years, the error cannot be corrected either. The damage done when someone is wrongly incarcerated for many years, cannot be undone. It will certainly leave ineradicable scars. Even worse, it may damage someone's life for good if he has been in jail for, let's say, thirty years, without being guilty.

Three: To execute justice is a very responsible task, and, as is the case with every action, certain risks are involved. We should never condemn a system because of the risks involved. We should consider the risks and reduce them to a minimum. Everyone who drives a car knows that he takes the risk of killing innocent people in an accident, and every year many *are* killed. Still no one says that therefore all traffic must stop, and no one declares that driving a car is unacceptable. To exercise justice and to execute capital punishment involves the risk that an innocent person may be convicted. However, considering the importance of the judicial system, the precautions taken to avoid mistakes, and the accuracy with which the courts are working, the "risk" that an innocent person may fall victim is minimal, especially when compared with the risk and the number of victims of traffic and other accidents. It is certainly not a sound ground for doing away with capital punishment.

d. *Is it cruel and inhuman?*

Capital punishment is considered to be cruel and inhuman, especially in a time when people almost everywhere are doing away with corporal punishment. Also this argument does not hold water, if we take a closer look at it. Of course, it can be done in a cruel way. Today many people are being tortured in countries all over the world. However, this happens even without the death penalty, and often the death penalty is less cruel than prolonged torture. Besides, let's not forget that an extended jail term can be horrifying and unbearable. If anything is inhuman, it is a life sentence. A human being, isolated in a cage, like an animal, is not really an elevating picture or a symbol of human dignity. It is quite well possible that a death penalty is more "humane" and less cruel than a life term in prison. Many criminals have stated that they would rather die than stay in jail for the rest of their lives. The argument of cruelty can certainly not be adduced in favour of a jail term and against capital punishment. Of course, the question remains in what way the punishment is executed. It may very well be that the electric chair is more cruel and torturous than the guillotine in the Middle Ages. But it is also possible to execute a death penalty without any torture or cruelty.

e. *Are we not allowed to kill?*

We are coming closer to the main point and the crucial question in this matter, and that is whether we have the right to kill in the first place. From a Christian point of view, some say, it is against the teaching of the New Testament. We have to love our neighbour and we have to forgive. However, to forgive and to love our neighbour does not contradict the necessity and obligation to exercise justice. The Bible certainly teaches us that we have to love our neighbour, but this love for the neighbour has to be shown also in doing justice according to the Word of God. We do not have the right to kill. That is clearly stated in the Bible. No individual person has the right to take away the life of someone else. However, the Bible also teaches us that the government does not bear the sword in vain. The death penalty is certainly not something that belongs only to the dispensation of the Old Testament. Romans 13 speaks very clearly about it. In Genesis 9:6 we read: "Whoever sheds the blood of man, by man shall his blood be shed; for God made man in His own image." That is a clear statement. And in Romans 13:4 we read: "For he [that is: the government] does not bear the sword in vain; he is the servant of God to execute His wrath on the wrongdoers." Some may say that the sword is mentioned only as the symbol of the power and authority given to the civil government. But the meaning is clear: although the sword may be a symbol, the purpose of the sword is to kill and to exercise justice by wielding the sword. The civil government, as the servant of God, has not only the right to take away life, but also the obligation to protect life, if necessary, by taking away the lives of those who kill others. It does not necessarily mean that the government has the *obligation* to exercise capital punishment with respect to *everyone* who, in one way or another, has taken away the life of someone else. It means, however, without any doubt, that the government has the *right* to execute the death penalty. As far as the obligation to execute this judgment is concerned, we will deal further with that in another section. For the time being, suffice it to say that the government has the *right* to take away human life.

f. *Is there no possibility of repentance?*

Some argue that capital punishment takes away the possibility of repentance and amendment of life. Especially from a Christian point of view we should try to convince a criminal of his wrongdoings and make him change his life and start again in obedience to the Lord. As long as someone is alive he can repent. Cutting off his life means that we, humanly speaking, remove any further possibility of repentance.

That sounds convincing. However, we should not be wiser than God. The Lord commands us to do justice, according to His Word, as we have stated above. In obedience to the Word of God we may count on His help, also in bringing a sinner to repentance. We don't know if and when someone will change his life. We know about a murderer on the cross who believed in Jesus Christ and was saved. Obedience to the Lord in the execution of the punishment He has prescribed will never cut off or limit the possibility of conversion, because it will never limit the work of the Holy Spirit. On the contrary. If someone is sentenced to death, the Holy Spirit can certainly use this fact to bring him to terms and make him change his attitude. The main point is that repentance and conversion is the work of the Holy Spirit and that disobedience to the Lord (in rejecting capital punishment) does not increase the possibility for the Holy Spirit to work. On the contrary. Only in obedience to the Word of God can we appeal to Him and His help.

So far our evaluation of the arguments against capital punishment. There are a number of general points which we have to consider before we can come to a balanced judgment in this matter. In the next section I will discuss some less sound arguments which are sometimes brought forward in favour of capital punishment. We will also deal with some aspects of punishment and corrective measures in general. In this way we will try to formulate our conclusions with respect to this issue.

4. Less pure arguments

Although I am convinced that capital punishment is in accordance with the Word of God, we have to be on the alert for some less pure arguments in this respect. There is always the danger that an element of revenge creeps in, and the Holy Scripture teaches us clearly that we should not avenge ourselves but leave it to the wrath of the Lord; for it is written, "Vengeance is mine, I will repay, says the Lord" (Romans 12:19).

Another aspect is the financial consequences. Some argue that life in prison costs the "taxpayer" a fortune. Are we supposed to spend so much money on criminals? Also this argument should never be decisive in making a decision in favour of or against capital punishment. The cost of imprisonment may play a role in the judicial system, but then in such a manner that ways and means are developed to make inmates do meaningful work to make up for the cost of their imprisonment. Without going to the extreme of so-called "penal servitude" or "hard labour camps," inmates can certainly be forced to spend their time in a meaningful way, to the benefit of society.

5. Corrective, remedial, or restorative

An aspect which deserves special attention is the notion that punishment should always be either corrective, remedial, or restorative. It should correct the wrong attitude of the convict, remedy his "disease," or restore the damage caused by his offence. In other words, it should serve a certain positive purpose and should not only be a matter of retaliation.

We have already seen that this point cannot be used especially against capital punishment, because it counts in general for every form of punishment. Besides, it is not true either that punishment always has to be corrective or restorative. Romans 13 teaches us clearly that the task of the government is to be the servant of God to execute His wrath on the wrongdoers (Romans 13:4). The punishment meted out by the civil government is certainly not only an educative matter. The Bible teaches us clearly that there is also an element of retaliation. That is why the punishment always has to be reasonable and in accordance with the character of the offence. Although retaliation does not pay back to the victim and does not restore the damage, it makes clear to the convict that he has to suffer as a consequence of his wrongdoings. Romans 13:4 says: "If you do wrong, be afraid, for he does not bear the sword in vain; he is the servant of God to execute His wrath on the wrongdoer."

Of course, punishment is not only retaliation. The aspect of correction and restoration has to be considered as well. The government should try to mete out the punishment in such a way that it can contribute to the rehabilitation of the offender. It should, if at all possible, be a remedial measure. But this aspect should not be the first and only one. Also restoration can be considered. There are cases nowadays where an offender is sentenced in such a manner that he can contribute to the restoration of the damage caused by his crime or that he can help to alleviate the suffering of the victims of his or someone else's wrongdoings.

6. Protection of the victims

A very important aspect of the judicial system is to protect the innocent. There is a tendency, or even a rule, to give the convict the benefit of the doubt. That might be right to a certain extent. No one should be sentenced without conclusive evidence. But it should never be at the cost of innocent victims. Sometimes very dangerous murderers are released on parole without sufficient precautions to protect potential victims, and it happens too often that more people are killed. That is not a matter of giving the criminal the benefit of the doubt. That is a matter of negligence on the part of the government. The innocent are not sufficiently protected against a well-known danger.

We are living in a time when everyone speaks about human rights, but one wonders why the "rights" of criminals are better protected than the rights of innocent victims and potential new victims. The Lord has given the civil government the mandate to maintain peace and order. He has given capital punishment, not to get rid of some bad people, but to protect human life against murderers.

7. Insanity

Nowadays many criminals, often also murderers, are discharged for reasons of insanity. What should our attitude be in this respect? We have to be careful with this designation. It is often used by a defence attorney to have his client released from further prosecution. The main point in this respect is whether the suspect can be accounted fully responsible for his actions. Two aspects have to be considered.

In the first place, it can happen that someone who is mentally ill or insane, hurts someone else or even causes someone else to die. It is clear that in such a case no capital punishment should be executed, but that medical treatment should be ordered. However, in how many cases of discharge for reasons of insanity is it really a matter of mental illness? It is often used by the defence to give the accused an easy way out and to provide him with an excuse for his crime. Having been released from prosecution the person often seems to be quite normal.

In the second place, if someone really is insane so that he kills his neighbour and poses a threat for the lives of others, he should be treated in an appropriate manner. He should be protected and prevented from doing such a terrible thing again. In such a situation no death penalty should be executed, but more than usual care should be given to the person to protect potential victims from being killed. That may necessitate very secure seclusion in an institution. Then we should not complain too much about the lack of freedom of the murderer (or the patient, if you wish), but we should first and foremost keep in mind the task of the government to protect people against a potential killer, either by a premeditated, deliberate action or by an outburst of an insane person.

8. Self-defence

A few remarks about killing in self-defence. We are not allowed to kill, but we are allowed to defend ourselves against a brutal attack.

In the Sermon on the Mount we read: "Do not resist one who is evil. But if any one strikes you on the right cheek, turn to him the other also." That does not mean that we are not allowed to defend our lives, our possessions, and the lives of our loved ones. It means that we are not supposed to act as judge in our own case and that we should suffer loss rather than to defend our own interests at any cost. We have to love our neighbour, even our enemy, and we have to be willing to give in and to humble ourselves. We have to regard others better than ourselves, and we have to accept loss rather than do harm to others.

The Bible teaches us clearly that we have to protect our house, our life, and all our possessions against robbers, burglars, and murderers. When someone, in an attempt to defend his own life, causes someone else to die, he does not commit murder. However, we have to be careful that our self-defence is in accordance with the danger and the character of the threat. Someone who protects his house with a security system that instantly kills any intruder, is still guilty of murder. It also makes quite a difference whether a civilian (a common citizen) kills an intruder, or that a police officer kills a criminal in an attempt to apprehend him during a shootout.

We should not be our own judge but leave it to the governing authorities to do justice. A matter of self-defence can easily become a matter of revenge. Even in Old Testament times, when the avenger was charged with the execution of capital punishment with respect to the murderer of his next-of-kin, six cities of refuge were selected and the manslayer could flee there when he had killed someone without intent.

9. An obligation to execute capital punishment?

The last point in this discussion is the question whether the government has the *duty* to execute capital punishment in every murder case. From what has been said it is perfectly clear that we believe that the government has the *right* to kill and that capital punishment is a Biblical way of dealing with murderers. Does that mean that every government that does not execute capital punishment in all cases of murder acts against the commandments of the LORD? Not necessarily. It all depends on the reason why or why not. The government, in the first place, has the task to maintain peace, order, and justice, to protect and defend the lives and the freedom of all citizens. In countries where capital punishment is still used (or was used in the past), it always is (or was) used only in very specific cases, often only for premeditated, deliberate killing, for so-called "first degree" murder, or for war criminals or traitors.

In our country a distiction is made between first and second degree murder, between manslaughter and criminal negligence which results in someone's death. It is clear that the death penalty would not be the proper punishment in all these cases. The government has a great responsibility in determining what the sentence should be. When it is perfectly clear that someone has deliberately killed innocent people, the only Scriptural punishment is the death penalty. I am convinced that a lot of violence and murder could have been prevented, if the governing authorities had been willing to act according to the Biblical rule, given in Genesis 9:6 and in Romans 13.

124

At the same time we have to realize that the Bible also teaches us about instances in which a criminal was granted mercy and was not put to death. Even Jesus Himself did so with the woman who, according to the law, had to be put to death. In some circumstances, for instance, in times of war and open revolution, there may be a greater necessity to execute capital punishment and there may be more instances in which it is the only way to execute justice. In normal circumstances, however, a jail term would be sufficient in many cases.

In each and every situation we have to recognize that neither our personal feelings of revenge, nor arguments of "humanity," should be decisive, but only what the Lord teaches us in His Word, and the responsibility, given to the governing authorities, to be God's servants for our good and to execute God's wrath on the wrongdoers (Romans 13:4).

CHAPTER TWELVE

Some Reflections on War and Disarmament

1. What is at stake?

The words *armament* and *army* are derived from a word that refers to tools, equipment, or weapons and the act of defending one's body and possessions by using these tools and weapons. However, when people nowadays use the words *army* and *armament*, they mean, in the first place, the activity of the government and the weapons used by the national (or international) defence organizations.

Dealing with questions about armament and disarmament is therefore, in the first place, a matter of dealing with the task of the government with respect to national defence. We must answer questions such as: What is the task of the civil government? Does the government have the right to use weapons which are ultimately meant to kill people, and then, in the case of nuclear weapons, on such a large scale? Are we only allowed to have a system of *defensive* weapons or is a government also allowed to employ *offensive* weapons in order to defend and protect its territory, if necessary, by attacking a potential or actual enemy on its own territory? What is the meaning of deterrence? Is the balance of terror system an acceptable way of preventing things from getting worse or is it too risky a balance? What should be our attitude with respect to unilateral nuclear disarmament?

Many more questions can be added to this list, and I do not pretend to have an answer to all of them. They are too complex to deal with exhaustively within the scope of this book. It is extremely important to consider these things, however. All around us we hear of actions and "peace movements." It is an ongoing process and it would be silly and irresponsible to ignore this development.

In this chapter we will pay attention to some aspects which may be forgotten or too often ignored, or at least are not taken into account enough.

We cannot solve the issues at stake with a simple yes or no, or by stating that we are in favour of or opposed to them. That is often the misleading way in which these thing are presented in an opinion poll. If you ask a thousand people whether they are in favour of or opposed to war, in favour of or opposed to the use of nuclear arms, in favour of or opposed to disarmament, they will all answer in the same way, at least if they have to list their answer statistically with a "yes or no." Still our judgment should be made more discriminatingly, because we have to consider the many aspects and implications of these matters.

2. The purpose of an army

In Romans 13 we read that the the governing authority is God's servant for our good. We have considered this in the previous chapter, dealing with capital punishment, and we have to keep it in mind also when we discuss the matter of armament and disarmament. The task of the government, in internal affairs, is to maintain peace and order in the country, to execute justice, and to protect the lives of all its citizens. With respect to foreign or external affairs, the government has the task to defend its citizens against a brutal attack by another country, to defend national independence and sovereignty.

We have seen that, in the event of a personal attack, self-defence is a dangerous matter. It can very easily lapse into revenge. The government, however, has the task to execute justice. It may even use the ultimate means of the death penalty to execute justice. With respect to external affairs the government has the task, if necessary, to use military forces to fulfil its mandate.

The Bible does not forbid war per se. We read that the people of Israel had to fight against their enemies and that the LORD gave detailed instructions for warfare. They even had to conquer the promised land and to annihilate its population. However, let us be careful with this example. The fact that the people of Israel conquered the promised land can never be used as a justification for the conquering of the territory of another country today. It was a very special situation; it was a special instruction given by the LORD for a specific purpose. No one may use it to justify his own actions. There is no special divine instruction in this respect any longer, not even for the present state of Israel.

However, what we can learn from the history narrated in the Old Testament is that a country has the right and the obligation to defend its national independence and its borders again intruders and against an attack by another nation. The Bible even teaches us that in defending our country we have to use logistic and strategic considerations, to avoid unnecessary casualties and risks. We should try to avoid a confrontation by negotiating, rather than fight a battle which we know is almost impossible to survive and to win. In Luke 14:31,32, we read the following words, spoken be our Lord Jesus Christ Himself: "What king, going to encounter another king in war, will not sit down first and take counsel whether he is able with ten thousand to meet him who comes against him with twenty thousand? And if not, while the other is yet a great way off, he sends an embassy and asks terms of peace."

From this example we can learn two things. In the first place, a government has the right to defend and protect its country and its national territory. In the second place, a government must consider the risk of losing the battle and must take appropriate measures to avoid an unnecessary risk of casualties.

Freedom is a precious gift from the Lord and worthy of being defended. The governing authority is given by the Lord to defend our national independence and the safety of our borders. A government has the right to call upon its citizens to serve in the army. A government has the right to use weapons and, if necessary, to kill in an effort to defend its national safety, either in a national defence system or in an international defence organization.

We have to obey the government also in this respect. Obedience to the government has a limit, however. When something is asked of us which brings us in direct conflict with the Word of God, we have to be more obedient to God than to man. In that case we should not follow the instruction of man — even if it results in great risks of punishment for our refusal to obey. However, in all other situations, in which the government does not ask us to act against the commandments of the Lord, we have to serve the governing authority, because the Lord has set them over us. We have to obey, even if we do not agree with the measures taken by the government, or when we do not understand the meaning or doubt the effectiveness of them. That is the basis of our obedience. A national defence system cannot work without obedience. If every person or every soldier has the right to determine whether a measure is correct and subsequently has the right to refuse obedience, the whole system will never work.

3. National independence

When we consider the task of the national government to defend its borders, we first have to say a few things about the character of these borders in general. In the Old Testament the LORD Himself set the national borders for His people Israel. In Proverbs 22:28 we read the warning: "Remove not the ancient landmarks which your fathers have set." This text is sometimes used to warn against changes in national borders. However, what counted for the borders of the promised land, which where set by the LORD Himself, cannot be applied to all the present national borders. The territory of the different nations today is not set by a divine revelation. It is often a matter of historical development. Of course, we can see the hand of the Lord in the historical developments. But there is also a factor of human responsibility, and even human mistakes. Not all national borders are established in the right way, that is, by justice and righteousness. Some are set by the use of force during a revolution. Some are the result of gross injustice and oppression or unwarranted conquering of territory. Still they become a historical reality, which cannot be ignored or undone. In politics we have to face reality, and the ideal situation is not always feasible. We have to live with the brokenness of society and the consequences of sin. To accept a certain existing situation as a reality is certainly not in conflict with Proverbs 22:28. The way in which a borderline came into existence might have been wrong, but we cannot deny its reality.

In the Second World War many nations fought for their independence and national sovereignty. Many were overtaken by the German army and became occupied territory. Fortunately the U.S.A. and Canada entered the battle and came to their rescue. They liberated the countries in Western Europe from the German occupation. As long as the war went on, the people in these countries had to fight for their lives and their freedom. That was a legitimate battle, including the underground organizations. However, if Germany would have won the battle, and no other nations had come to the rescue of the Western European countries, they would have been incorporated in the German territory. That would have been very sad, and we must be thankful to the Lord that He prevented such a disaster. But if it would have happened, we would have had to face that reality.

Note what happened in Eastern Europe. The borders of the Soviet Union were not all established in a democratic way. The different countries in that part of the world are not all independent, and some have even lost their national identity or existence. Take, for instance, the Balkan States and the whole process of "Balkanization." We can condemn and deplore this development — and we certainly do — but it is nevertheless a reality. Think also about the present development in Poland and Afghanistan.

Nowadays many new states are coming into existence through a coup d'état or a revolution. The way in which a state comes into existence and the way the borders are set is not always correct or justifiable. Still it is reality. When such a situation has existed for a while and is settled, it becomes a historical fact. We cannot ignore it. The borderlines are there and will gradually be recognized by almost all countries.

There are two reasons why I mention these things and elaborate on them quite extensively. In the first place, to make clear that we should not just take it for granted that we live in a free country. We have to accept it as a gift from the Lord and we have to be thankful for it. In the second place, to show that our freedom and national independence are worth defending. We can lose them if we are not on the alert and if we do not fight for them.

With respect to the so-called occupied countries and territories, they may regain their independence and freedom by using all legitimate means to the utmost of their power. At the same time they have to be obedient to the governing authority, as long as it does not bring them in conflict with the revealed Word of God. The rule of the Word of God, given in Romans 13, holds also with respect to a government which is not righteous and just in every respect. In I Peter 2:18 we read: "Servants, be submissive to your masters with respect, not only to the kind and gentle, but also to the overbearing." And the apostle Paul did not write about the governing authority in his letter to the Romans in a time when they were ruled by a Christian government or by a righteous ruler. He wrote to people who lived under the rude and usurpatious government of the Roman Caesar. The main part of his territory was "occupied" country. Still the apostle exhorts his readers to respect and obey the governing authorities.

All this should be a strong incentive for us to be very careful and on the alert to defend the freedom and independence given to us by the Lord under His divine providence. It bring us to the central issue, namely, national defence.

4. National defence

We have seen in the previous section that national bounderies are not unchangeable entities. They are not based upon a divine revelation, as was the case with the people of Israel in the time of the Old Testament. Neither are they subject to the prohibition mentioned in Proverbs 22:28: "Remove not the ancient landmarks which your fathers have set." National bounderies can be changed, and they have changed quite often. Such changes are a reality, even if they take place in a way which cannot be approved. We cannot deny or ignore a historical development or an actual situation, whether we agree with it or not.

At the same time we have to be aware of our responsibility with regard to the existing situation. We should see and consider our freedom and the existence of our country within its present bounderies as a gift from the hand of the Lord. The historical development took place under His providence. That does not exclude human failures and mistakes and human responsibility. But it makes us very thankful for the rich blessing we can enjoy.

In oppression and persecution the Lord takes care of His people. That is a comfort for those who have forfeited their freedom and are living under the burden of persecution, dictatorship, occupation, or even worse. At the same time we should take care that we do not lose our freedom and independence through our own negligence. We have the opportunity to serve the Lord without hindrance. That is a great privilege. Let us be careful that we do not forfeit these gifts. They are worth fighting for.

The task of the government is to restrain the evil one, to promote justice and peace, and to protect the country, as we have seen in the previous chapter. We noted that the government has to do justice when crimes are committed and that it may even be warranted to use the death penalty. In international relationships there is an analogy. The government has to defend human life and freedom against oppressors and killers, even by using lethal weapons when necessary.

The Bible does not forbid warfare per se. The question is whether a certain war is justifiable and whether appropriate means are used to limit the number of casualties as much as possible.

With respect to national strategy and the actions of the police force in dealing with criminals, we all agree that in a case of "hit-and-run" the police should not immediately shoot the suspect, but try to apprehend him in a more peaceful way. When an unidentified airplane intrudes into our airspace, it can be forced to make a landing, but a passenger plane which goes off course should not be destroyed, as recently happened with a Korean Boeing 747.

The civil government has the duty to defend the country and national sovereignty against every brutal attack by a potential or actual enemy. That means that a defense system has to be built up and that agreements can be made with other nations to cooperate and to protect each other's territory. Such a defense system has to be *adequate* and *appropriate*.

What do I mean by *adequate* and *appropriate*? Let me try to explain.

Adequate means that the army has to be capable of fulfilling its task. The manpower and the weaponry has to fit the circumstances. There should be enough strength and determination to hold off the enemy. Let us not underestimate this aspect. Only a strong defence will prevent a war and keep the enemy from going too far. A weak defence system will never be respected by a potential attacker.

The defence system should also be *appropriate*. The meaning of this word is similar to that of the previous one, but there is an essential difference. *Appropriate* means that you do not use a cannon to kill a mosquito. When, for instance, a border needs to be defended against guerrilla fighters and intruders who are working on an individual basis, it does not make much sense and it is not appropriate to use heavy artillery, tanks, and bombers. Smaller-scale weaponry should be used and would be more appropriate. By the same token, it would be inappropriate to use handguns when the enemy comes with heavy tanks.

5. Deterrence

What has been said in the previous section brings us to the conclusion that for the buildup of a defence system decisions must be made as to what kind of weapons will be adequate and appropriate. However, the problem is that you never know exactly what kind of attack you will be faced with. Therefore, in principle, the army has to be prepared for every possible situation. For practical reasons this is virtually impossible. It would also be too expensive.

Besides, there is a saying that an ounce of prevention is better than a pound of cure. The first and foremost goal of the army should be to prevent war. Remember the words of our Lord Jesus Christ in Luke 14:31,32 about a king who, before he encounters another king in battle, first sits down and takes counsel to see whether his army is strong enough to win the battle or whether it might be better to avoid a confrontation by negotiating a settlement.

There are different methods of keeping the enemy from attacking a country. There is a Latin expression, *Si vis pacem, para bellum.* That means: If you want peace, be prepared for war. One method of preventing an attack is to show such superiority in manpower and weaponry that no enemy dares to start a war. That is a very expensive way. At the same time there has to be enough determination. If a country has a large arsenal of weapons and a large army but everyone knows that they are simply not prepared to use them, for whatever reason that may be, the system does not work and no enemy will be deterred by it. If you want peace, be prepared for war! Most wars have been triggered by the attacker's conviction that he could easily win the battle.

The question is: How far do we go in this respect? There is always a risk involved, regardless of which approach we take. Too weak a defence system makes a country vulnerable, but too strong an army is a waste of money. Moreover, too strong a defence system can trigger an escalation in the arms race, as we will see in the next section.

When I say that too weak a defence system makes a country vulnerable and invites trouble, I do not mean that it necessarily will lead to a war or an open attack by an enemy. Most troubles these days are caused by an unwillingness to negotiate and by all kinds of local and small-scale provocations. The willingness of the Eastern European countries to negotiate and to come to any concession in disarmament talks depends completely on the determination of the Western defence systems. The developments in Poland, Hungary, Afghanistan, the Middle East, and many other parts of the world depend largely on the deterrent effect of the Western defence organizations.

However, a deterrent effect works only if there is the ultimate willingness to use the army with all its weaponry, if necessary. That brings us to a very critical issue: the balance of terror.

6. Balance of terror

One of the methods of keeping a potential enemy from attacking a country is to build up an army with a clear superiority in manpower as well as in weaponry. However, that inevitably leads to escalations in the arms race. Overkill capacity and military superiority of the one superpower will force the other into a desperate attempt to catch up on its defensive power. Also in this respect we have to consider the aspect of appropriateness. If the one becomes superior, the other will feel "attacked" and will build up and expand his defence system at any cost. That is what has happened in recent decades and is still going on.

After the Second World War the U.S.A. was certainly superior to the Soviet Union with respect to its military power. However, the Soviet Union did not trust this situation. Let us not forget that their attitude and philosophy are completely different from ours. They simply do not believe that a superior America will not use its position to attack them or at least abuse its position to get its way at the cost of the Soviet Union and their political goals. As the saying goes: Ill-doers are ill-deemers. They expect others to act in the same way as they themselves would. The Soviet Union has set its goals and will try to reach these goals with all available means. They are prepared to accept a policy of "détente" if it is in the interests of their ultimate goal. They are also prepared to use their military superiority if it can serve their purpose. We have seen clear examples in recent history that they do not hesitate to use their army if they consider it useful, in spite of public opinion. Their policy is opportunistic, devoid of many moral and ethical considerations. Therefore the military superiority of the Western countries was absolutely unacceptable for them. At all costs they have tried (and have succeeded) to reach at least a balance.

By the same token the U.S.A. cannot accept being in an inferior position. They are also convinced that the Soviet Union, on their part, would abuse such a situation. In this way a so-called "balance of terror" has been reached. The fact that both are so strong that neither one of them can win a battle, keeps them from starting a war or using their weapons against each other. This balance of terror has worked quite well over the last decades. There have been different occasions when a show of power and determination has caused even the Soviet Union to back off. However, there are at least two dangerous aspects to this matter which we should consider.

In the first place, it is difficult to determine whether a real "balance" exists. Who can find out what the strength of either party is? Who can tell how exact the "balance" is? The whole military system is built upon the principle of secrecy. The intelligence agencies do not always work perfectly. Espionage and counterespionage is a difficult business with many mistakes and risks involved.

In the second place, such a "balance," if it really exists, can easily be disturbed. Who should be put together on either side of the balance? In the past, the military power of the Soviet Union and China might have been put together on one side with the power of the U.S.A. and its Western allies on the other. In recent years, however, the relationship between the Soviet Union and China has been of such a nature that they certainly are not prepared to be put together. There have even been accusations that China was working together *with* the U.S.A. *against* the Soviet Union. That disturbs the whole idea of a balance of power and terror. The fact that more nations in the southern hemisphere are becoming relatively independent, also creates a new situation. Take, for instance, the development in the Central and South American countries as well as in Central and South Africa. To which side of the balance are they to be added? It is quite well possible that in the future there will be not just two but more "superpowers," and that makes the balance of terror even more unstable.

There is more we must consider. A balance of terror inevitably causes an escalation of the arms race. Because no one is sure exactly how strong the enemy is, they all try to be on the safe side, just a little stronger than the other. That makes the situation even more dangerous. This vicious circle has to be broken before it is too late, before it runs completely out of control. In the present situation the defence system is so complicated and sophisticated that no human being is able to consider all the implications of a certain move within a reasonable period of time. Very important decisions about life and death would have to be taken within minutes. Therefore computers have to be involved. But there is an increasing chance that errors will be made, that wrong assessments of a certain situation will set in motion a process which cannot be stopped. The balance of terror is based on a system of counterattack within a few minutes. One mistake can have disastrous and catastrophic consequences. A false alarm can trigger an attack, and who will be able to stop it? That is why the superpowers have come to the conclusion that the vicious circle must be broken. It is a matter of "to be or not to be" for all parties involved. The possibility of arms reduction or disarmament must be considered.

7. Disarmament

Seeing the results of the arms talks and the hesitation of both super-powers to make concessions, one might wonder why they started these talks in the first place. The answer is simply that they had to. It was a must! Both sides realized that the arms race and the balance of terror were running out of control. The reactions and the resistance of public opinion also had to be faced.

At disarmament conferences the participants function according to the same rule which determines the arms race, and that is the question how far they trust each other and are convinced of each other's determination to face the consequences. Also at these meetings the effect of deterrence works. If the parties at a disarmament conference make wrong assessments with respect to each other's determination, how will the system of deterrence ever work when a real confrontation takes place? Therefore these arms talks are extremely important; the results, humanly speaking, are decisive for the political and military developments of the near future.

Of course, both sides try to show off and win favour with the public. It is a big propaganda campaign. Both are more eager to win public support than we realize. Every move is well-considered. The Soviet Union is also really concerned about public opinion.They cannot afford to continue the arms race as it is today. It may very well kill their own economy. We don't know too much about what is going on behind the Iron Curtain, but even a dictatorial regime can spend a ruble only once. People need food to live, and making people slaves of the system has its limits. The Soviet Union has tried desperately and has succeeded in catching up with the U.S.A. in the arms race, but don't ask what it has cost the national economy, which is in very bad shape in spite of very ambitious plans.

The Soviet Union is not prepared to give up its ultimate goals, but it is necessary, also for them, to bring the escalation in the arms race to a halt.

It is important therefore, that we strive and fight for multilateral disarmament. It is in the best interests of all the parties involved. But it can be reached only with the determination and willingness to face realty.

8. Unilateral disarmament

Many people are so frightened by the prospect of nuclear war that they talk about unilateral disarmament. Their reasoning goes like this: if we show our willingness to stop the arms race by throwing away our weapons, in the first place all nuclear weapons, the Soviet Union will see that we mean business. They will not feel threatened any longer and they will follow suit. In this way we can restore mutual trust and peace in this world.

Unfortunately, this is a rather naive attitude. It does not take into consideration the completely different approach and way of thinking of people in the Eastern European countries. They have a different philosophy and attitude than we have. The people in the Kremlin do not feel the same as we do. They simply do not believe that someone would give up his defence and trust someone else. Instead, they consider unilateral disarmament to be a matter of weakness and lack of determination. They will only take advantage of the situation to reach their own goal. We also have to consider the big propaganda campaign. According to some people who have escaped the Soviet system and have first-hand knowledge, the Soviet Union is working very hard to promote the so called "peace" movements in the world. Every action opposing nuclear armament and in favour of unilateral disarmament is applauded by them. They are even willing to support these movements financially, wherever possible. At the same time they would never allow such actions in their own country.

It is unfortunate that many "peace" activists are not aware of the fact that they are being manipulated. The whole worldwide peace movement is certainly a political matter, and a big propaganda project as well. Many activists are manipulated by naively following the propaganda, while others are actively involved in this manipulation of public opinion. This is a very dangerous situation. It can destroy or at least do great damage to the deterrent effect of our defence organizations and the balance of terror. Instead of bringing peace it increases the chance that a local conflict causes a restricted war. Let us be realistic. The Soviet Union is not yet prepared to take the risk of a worldwide nuclear war. And they will never have to if the development continues as it is today. The undermining of the Western defence system by all kinds of "peace" movements will give them military superiority anyway. They do not even have to increase their arsenal to reach their goal, and they do not have to use their missiles.

The greatest danger today is not a well-considered nuclear attack. Of course, it could happen through a complicated process of human mistakes, computer errors, miscalculations, and misinterpretations. However, an even greater danger is that the Soviet Union, because of its superiority in the arms race, will try to reach its goal via small steps, as in Poland, Afghanistan and other parts of the world.

As it is today, they can take it easy and just go step by step. It doesn't involve too much of a risk, because the Western world is disunited and unable to resist them. Public opinion prevents the Western world from taking firm actions and from showing real determination. That basically means the end of the balance of terror.

Unless we are aware of these developments, we cannot make a sound assessment of what is going on today. Unilateral disarmament does not solve any problems. On the contrary, it makes matters worse and gives to the Soviet Union and its allies the advantage.

9. Are nuclear weapons acceptable?

In spite of all we have said up till now, there is still the question: Are nuclear weapons acceptable? Although part and parcel of the arms race and of the balance of terror, is it an acceptable and appropriate tool in this respect?

From recent publications, we all know that a full-scale nuclear war will leave no survivors and no real winners. The bombing of Hiroshima and Nagasaki at the end of the Second World War had a terrible aftermath. The present nuclear weapons are much more potent. There is a great overkill capacity. A nuclear war will leave no life on earth untouched, and what will be left may hardly appear to be life. It is a totally inhuman method of warfare.

Certainly, that is true. Such a war would almost annihilate human life from the earth. No one can deny or ignore this reality. But yet, more has to be said to give a complete picture of all the aspects involved in nuclear armament. The atom bombs dropped on Japan created a terrible ordeal, but many more casualties and cruelties would have taken place in the Japanese concentration camps if the war had dragged on for many more years.

During the last forty years, or at least part of them, the presence of nuclear weapons on both sides, humanly speaking, has kept both superpowers from using them. If the U.S.A. would have destroyed all its nuclear weapons and would have stopped further development, would the Soviet Union have done the same? I doubt it very much. If the Soviet Union would have had the monopoly in this respect, do you think that they would not have used their power? I'm not sure. At least they would have used their tactical nuclear weapons in local conflicts to bring matters to a fast solution and to achieve their own goals. They would have used their superiority to reach their goals everywhere.

The presence of nuclear weapons on both sides has prevented their use.

And yet the question remains: Can we and may we use as a deterrent weapons which never will be used.? If someone has a gun, but everyone knows that he will never use it, it does not have any effect as a deterrent. The balance of power is effective only if both parties are prepared to use their weapons. In the military strategy of the U.S.A. the use of nuclear weapons is certainly included as an option. Dangerous as this might be, it is the only way to prevent things from getting worse.

We have to face the reality that these weapons exist. Throwing away all Western nuclear weapons would only increase the danger that the Soviet Union will use them. Though deterrence and the balance of terror might be frightening, the absence of this balance would be even worse.

Some reason: "Let us, unilaterally, start with a nuclear disarmament and the Soviet Union will follow suit." I am convinced they will not, as I have stated before. Some argue that it would be better to live under Soviet supremacy than to face the possibility of a nuclear war. That may sound reasonable. But is it realistic? People who have escaped the Soviet Union have a different opinion. The communist system will never halt its efforts to gain power everywhere. Even the people at the top do not trust each other and are sometimes prepared to kill one another to reach their personal goals, as history has proved. The power struggle in the Kremlin is not a public matter. It does not go like an election campaign in our part of the world. But if that is how things are among "comrades" in the Kremlin, let us not have any illusions about the grassroots. Our freedom and independence are at stake and they are worth defending.

Besides, for us as Christians there is another point we have to consider. In our Western part of the world we can serve the Lord without hindrance. Let us be thankful for that. The communist system takes away this freedom. Of course, we know that the Lord takes care of His people, also in persecution. But we should not willingly allow ourselves to be brought into such a situation. We have to be careful not to forfeit our privileges.

10. Eschatological perspective

There is one more aspect that must be mentioned.

What has been said so far seems to paint a gloomy picture of the future. Is a third world war inevitable? Many, in an irresponsible, naive manner, follow the leaders of the "peace" movements. People seem to be willing to give up their freedom. Where will this all end? Does the future hold a global destruction or an atheistic supremacy . . . and worldwide persecution of the church?

We have to look at it in a different way! In the first place, it may very well be that a war or global disaster is at hand. It is also possible that a time of persecution of the church is coming. But basically we have known that all along. The Bible, in many places, tells us about war, persecution, and global calamities. But such catastrophies will not occur because of human mistakes, nor through a well-thought-out attack by an enemy. They will come as a fulfilment of prophecy.

It is not a decision of a superpower or a computer error that will cause the destruction of this world and the end of all human life, but the sound of the trumpet and the word of our Lord will trigger a great calamity. That will be the great eschatological event, the renewal of this earth at Christ's glorious return.

We do not know what means the Lord will use to bring this earth to an end. Our heavenly Father has very often used sinful actions of men to bring His plan of salvation to its fulfilment. He will do so also in the future. Let us not lose heart.

We have to face our responsibility to defend our country, our freedom and our national independence and sovereignty. Ultimately, we know that we are citizens of the Kingdom of Heaven, from where we expect our Saviour and our King.

Let us work, being fully aware of our responsibility. Let us fulfil our mandate in this world. Don't worry too much.

If we have done what we can do, the Lord will do what we cannot do. Our life is in His hand. The whole world is under His supremacy. He is the one and only real "Superpower." In His care and under His protection we are safe.